10101010101
MICRO Series

W9-DEN-922

202+

SOFTWARE
PACKAGES

TO USE IN YOUR LIBRARY

*Descriptions, Evaluations,
and Practical Advice*

Patrick R. Dewey

AMERICAN LIBRARY ASSOCIATION

Chicago and London 1992

Cover and text designed by Charles Bozett

Composed by Alexander Typesetting, Inc. in Times Roman and Helvetica on Datalogics

Printed on 50-pound Finch Opaque, a pH-neutral stock, and bound in 10-point C1S cover stock by IPC

The paper used in this publication meets the minimum requirements of American National Standard for Information Sciences—Permanence of Paper for Printed Library Materials, ANSI Z39.48-1984. ∞

Library of Congress Cataloging-in-Publication Data

Dewey, Patrick R., 1949–
    202 + software packages to use in your library : descriptions, evaluations, and practical advice / by Patrick R. Dewey.
        p. cm.—(101 micro series)
    Rev. ed. of: 101 software packages to use in your library, 1987.
    Includes bibliographical references and index.
    1. Libraries—Automation—Computer programs. 2. Microcomputers—Library applications—Computer programs. 3. Library science—Computer programs. I. Dewey, Patrick R., 1949– 101 software packages to use in your library. II. Title. III. Title: Two hundred two plus software packages to use in your library. IV. Title: Two hundred and two plus software packages to use in your library. V. Series.
Z678.9.A3D483 1992
025'.02'0285536—dc20   91-42688

Printed in the United States of America.

96 95 94 93 92   5 4 3 2 1

This book is for
my two dogs,
Printer and Software,
and in memory of my dog Hardware,
whom I miss very much

Contents

Introduction

Much has happened since *101 Software Packages* was published in 1986. That book was an honest effort to obtain and examine over 100 software packages, both to summarize factual data and to make some evaluative comments. Some people may think that *101 Software Packages* should have contained more software, but it is very difficult to get any group of people or corporations to return 101 of anything. Even when the software package is in hand, it can take an enormous amount of time to evaluate the software properly.

I was fortunate that 202 + SOFTWARE PACKAGES was not twice as difficult to write as its predecessor, for several reasons. First, the success of the first book made producers less reluctant to send copies. Also, more software is available from which to choose, generally of better quality than in 1985 and 1986.

This volume contains more than 256 packages, but we liked the title 202 better, whatever the actual count, so we kept it. The next version, scheduled for two years from now, may be called *303 Microcomputer Software Packages*. I will try to find enough new packages to make such a title truthful. With each new version, I try to expand the other features in the volume, making it more useful. I have been particularly gratified by those librarians who have commented favorably thus far; *101 Software Packages* seems to have been very well received.

The goal of the present book is to provide an easy and convenient way for librarians to begin their search for software. I have tried to be much more thorough than I was in compiling the first version. To this end, more than twice as many software packages are included.

Data on the software reviewed in this volume came from two basic sources. Much information was found during a literature search; practicing librarians chose a software package to do some particular task in their library and reported on it in the literature. The remainder of the programs reviewed was chosen from materials found to be available or advertised. Hundreds of letters requesting review copies were then sent to vendors.

All of the software in this book was judged to be of value to somebody for some task or system in a library. Programs with only negative reviews were ignored, software that was grossly deficient or inappropriate for library work was not included.

This book has several objectives. One is to provide enough detailed information about library-relevant software to allow practicing librarians to seek out and identify packages of use to them. Another objective is to provide reviews of packages within each category. While, for example, it was not possible to provide a review of every catalog card production system, I looked at enough of them to be able to give evaluative insights into what to look for when considering one for purchase.

Any book—any source of information—about software is simply a place to start.

A Computer System: Hardware, Software, and People

As a teacher at Rosary College in River Forest, Illinois, for the past five years, I have been fond of telling my students that a computer system comprises hardware, software, and people. My point in such a statement is to emphasize "people," since they are the part of the equation that is often overlooked. People are the important part in more than one way. People have feelings and need safety from the elements. They also think and have motivations. If they are not treated as an important part of the computer system, they may let the whole microcomputer project die. On the other hand, if the right people are given the right type of administrative support, they can take a computer system project to undreamed-of heights. It is the people, also, that the system must start with, for they must select the software and the hardware. I have never heard of a project or library in which the computer selected the people.

Successful computerization means discussing the project with the staff, getting input, and coming to a consensus. One motivated staffer, given the right support, will come forward when problems arise. I believe the best principle for computerization, no matter what size or type of library, is to ask each department head to brainstorm with his or her staff. Suddenly, the whole project is on their shoulders, and rightfully so. They should ask themselves: Do we want a microcomputer? If yes, what will we use it for? Their answers will take into account hardware, software, and people.

From staff interviews and meetings, a written assessment of needs can then be prepared.

Hardware

There is an easy and clear distinction between hardware and software. Hardware can be touched—the monitor, disk drives, chips, and other physical parts. Software, on the other hand, is the intangible instructions. In this distinction, a disk is hardware, but the instructions contained on it are software, much like the cells of the brain and the thoughts contained therein.

Though it is overly simplistic to say so, the world has become divided into three basic groups of microcomputer users: IBM (or compatibles), the Apple II family, and the Macintosh. The primary consideration in the selection of a microcomputer is not the computer itself, but the strength of the various components which we shall discuss below. The purchase of a certain computer may sometimes be more of a political decision than a practical one, since people (and corporations) develop certain prejudices towards hardware. It can be seen as subversive in some quarters to purchase the ''wrong'' type of machine.

Another valid reason for purchasing a particular type of computer is that it can be convenient to have the same kind of computer throughout an office or organization. The computer and its components are then easy to exchange, and you can understand each other better since you have only one computer's jargon with which to contend.

Obviously, with the addition of peripherals and extensions, it is possible to increase the power of almost any computer to a very significant degree. In the end, with politics and other things being equal, the librarian must decide how much money can be spent and what type of computer will do the job. An Apple II that has been enhanced with memory boards and powerful peripherals may have much more power than a stripped-down IBM, but more and more people are shying away from the use of an Apple II for any but educational or public access use. Fewer libraries are choosing this computer, even though it may be all that some small libraries would ever need and it is less intimidating and easier to use. Whether or not the Apple II will eventually be replaced with a series of low-end Macintosh computers remains to be seen. Currently, they are still a good buy. For many small libraries, they will still do the job very effectively.

IBM has the name as the leading business microcomputer. Much sophisticated and advanced software exists for doing spreadsheet analysis and word processing. The leading word processor, *WordPerfect*, is IBM-based. Excellent spreadsheets for the IBM abound. A library or a department may need this level of computing.

The Macintosh is in a class all by itself. It cannot be beaten when it comes to graphics and desktop publishing. Libraries that use a microcomputer exclusively for publications would be wise to consider a Macintosh.

Beyond choosing specific machines for specific tasks, some libraries will want to standardize their computers, and there is something to be said for having only one type of microcomputer. It is, however, not impossible to manage well with several different systems.

Even when the type of computer to purchase has been decided, the library staff must still decide what size hard disk drive, RAM, modem, printer, and other peripherals are required. In the case of the IBM-PC, for example, there are now so many clones (or compatibles) that it may take some time just to analyze which one is best.

The selection of the hardware package must begin with the staff's needs assessment. (Again, the people part of the equation must be analyzed.) If the library already owns hardware, a reexamination of equipment may reveal aspects which may be enhanced. In either case, questions such as how many microcomputers to buy, how much memory is needed, how powerful the disk drives should be, and what input devices, printers, and modems are needed must all be considered.

How Computers Work

To put things as simply as possible, computers are electronic; they count very fast. The computer's basic and most important job is to count, to compare its count with its internal ASCII code, and to report the results to the operator.

The fundamental component of the computer is the silicon wafer or chip upon which the computer information is manipulated. A circuit board is a collection of chips with connecting pathways. There are usually several of these in any particular computer. Often a circuit board is used to control a specific device such as a printer or a modem.

On the silicon chips are tiny intangible bits, or binary digits, of computer thought: *1*s and *0*s. A bit is either electrically charged (positive), or it is not (negative). If the bit is positive, it is a *1*. If it is negative, it is *0*.

Eight or more bits are grouped together in a byte, and the bytes are used to form a code. A code represents an alphabet of numbers and letters and other symbols. All computers understand one particular code, which is the American Standard Code for Information Interchange (ASCII), although other codes are used as well.

Bytes are generated in order to produce information. As these bytes add up, they are counted as kilobytes or *K*s (thousands of bytes), megabytes (millions of bytes), and gigibytes (billions of bytes). All of this information is termed software.

Depending on the software information travels in one of two ways in digital electronics. When it travels in eight separate paths simultaneously, it is called parallel transmission. When it travels single file in only one path, it is termed serial transmission.

Computers store information in the same manner as it is generated. Every separate collection of information is termed a file. The file may be stored internally, either temporarily in random-access memory (RAM) or permanently in read-only memory (ROM). Files may also be stored externally on a disk drive. A software package may consist of one or many files on one or more floppy diskettes, a hard-disk drive, or even a CD-ROM, a mass storage device that houses many megabytes. External storage is an important component in the selection of a complete computer system.

Input Devices.   Input devices are necessary to add data to the microcomputer. Chief among these is the keyboard. Different style keyboards exist. The

Macintosh, for example, now offers an expanded keyboard similar to the IBM keyboard. A mouse, a small handheld device, is another input device. It bypasses the keyboard to quickly move the cursor on the monitor. A scanner, another input device, inputs whole documents into the computer without redrawing or keyboarding them.

Another thing that computers do very well is to talk or communicate directly with each other. A modem is both an input and output device that makes data available to a computer. It allows two computers to communicate with each other. Two modems, one on each computer, and a telephone line are required along with special software. The first modem takes the digital code of the first computer and converts it to the analog (modulating) code of the telephone system. The telephone line then transmits the signal to its destination, another computer. The second modem, at that computer, converts the signal back into digital code, which the computer can understand. The signal has been modulated and then demodulated—hence, *modem*.

A facsimile transmitter (or fax) is a form of modem. Special hardware converts the document to be sent, or faxed, into an analog wave and sends it through a telephone line. The fax machine (or specially equipped computer) at the other end translates it back again.

Output Devices.   Information from the computer is read by the user with an output device. The most frequently used output device is the computer screen, or monitor. Screens are now available in black and white, green, amber, and other colors. For the highest resolution picture, it may be necessary to purchase a more expensive monitor. Color circuit cards and monitors may be required depending upon the software and the requirements of the user.

After the screen, or monitor, a printer is perhaps the most popular output device. Information generated by the printer is also called hardcopy. To print from the computer, material is routed to the printer with special commands.

Important here is the difference between types of printers. The most commonly used has been the relatively inexpensive dot matrix printer, often called simply a DMP. This type of printer uses a small matrix of needles to print dots, which then combine to form characters. These printers have progressed in sophistication through the years so that now they rival the next most popular printer, the letter-quality printer. Sometimes called the daisywheel printer, the letter-quality printer uses a spinning wheel made up of spokes. Each spoke has a different letter, and the printer forms characters by striking these spokes with a very tiny hammer. This is the same method used by most typewriters today, and it produces print as good as a typewriter. The only drawback to letter-quality printers is that they are typically slower than other kinds of printers. They also cannot print graphics, something at which the DMP excels.

Another type of printer, the inkjet printer, squirts a small jet of ink onto the paper to form characters. It can produce color as well.

The best printers available today are laser printers. They are much more expensive than the other types of printers, but they can produce materials of professional quality. A laser printer, sometimes called a page printer, will produce an entire page of copy at one time, instead of a character or line at a time, as dot or letter-quality printers do.

Choosing Computer Hardware

There are many aspects to the selection and purchase of a microcomputer system. The most common caveat is to not start with the hardware, but, first, to determine your needs, find software that fits those needs, and then choose the hardware that uses that software. This sequence sounds very clear and straightforward, but, in fact, it can rarely be done that way.

For instance, a small library may need a microcomputer to automate its production of catalog cards. Producing catalog cards may be the only function to which the computer will be put, since the department may need it a lot for that purpose. It then makes sense to look for the best catalog card production software that fits the needs of the department. The system may not require a hard-disk drive, since the catalog card data is not usually saved once the cards have been printed out. The system may also not require a color monitor or much internal memory. In other words, it may be possible in this instance for the library to get along with a minimal computer. In this simple scenario, there is one catch, catalog cards are printed on heavy stock. Most printers cannot accommodate this paper, since it drags on the printer's platen. It is possible, however, to purchase a bottom-feed printer. Card stock is fed through the bottom of the printer, thereby not wrapping the paper around the platen. This library will need to first consider the printing capabilities in choosing a system.

In another scenario, a much larger library may need to decide on the type of circulation system to purchase. This library will have to estimate how many linked terminals will be needed to support the circulation. An adequately large hard-disk drive will be needed. Printers for overdue notices, and much more will have to be considered. Here again the hardware is an important consideration in the decision.

Finally, many libraries may already have much in the way of hardware. For these libraries, add-on hardware, such as more or larger disk drives and better printers will be an important consideration.

The maintenance of hardware is vital once the system is in place. Most computers will not require a lot of maintenance. There may be a computer center or outlet not far away, and the computers can be taken to them whenever necessary. Other maintenance considerations include keeping the computer away from excessive heat, moisture, and smoke. Diskettes are also very sensitive to magnets, and a jolt of electricity can cripple both hardware and software. A simple way to defuse this potential problem is to provide a surge protector for all equipment.

Ergonomics, the physical comfort and safety of the staff, is also an important consideration. Excessive monitor glare, heat, or cold can affect the staff's comfort and performance.

Theft prevention must be considered. Several ways exist to tighten security around the machines. Special cables can be attached to keep the casual thief from taking equipment. Security pads can be used for the same thing. Computers should never be left in an unwatched area of the library.

Software

How Software Works

As discussed in the previous section on hardware, bits are gathered into bytes and the computer interprets these as instructions and data, making up software, the intangible information generated by the computer.

Software is ultimately the result of the addition of binary digits, or bits. Bits translate into the ASCII code. With programming languages, the computer can also be told to do certain things with the information. There are several types of language, including assembly language, which is very close to the natural way in which the machine communicates. The machine uses machine language, but assembly language is a shorthand form that is easier for humans to understand.

High-level languages include COBOL, BASIC, FORTRAN and many others. They are the languages in which most software programming is done. BASIC, an acronym for basic all-purpose symbolic instruction code, was the first important language and was developed for educational purposes.

One major software program is the disk operating system, or DOS. The IBM program interfaces between the user and the microcomputer, allowing the use of peripherals, the hard-disk drive, files, and much more. The Macintosh operating system provides much the same services, but it uses an entirely different method, one based on icons or graphic images, and is called the graphic user interface, or GUI.

The major type of software in use is applications software. This type of software performs a specific function without requiring much programming. Applications software includes catalog card and bibliography production, word processing, and spreadsheets. It is applications software that librarians—and all professionals—must learn to select and use.

Types of Software Information

Information describing software comes as basic facts, opinions, and testimonials. The basic facts cover such things as how many records the program will hold, how fast it will sort, who makes it, how much memory is required to run it, how much it costs, and so on. Opinions are usually written reviews; reviewers look at a demonstration or sample package and then write their opinions about it. The only real trouble with opinions is that the reviewers may not have the same criteria for evaluation as the people reading the review. For instance, the reviewer may be from a research library while the reader may be from a school library.

Finally, testimonials are accounts from people who have actually used the package. These usually come from librarians in the field. By calling up a library using a particular package, a purchaser can often get an opinion or help, although it may not be easy. Calling libraries to see if they have a package you are interested in can take some time. A short cut is the union list of software developed by some libraries. This simple survey of hardware and software, indexed by title, reveals what library is using what software in a particular area.

Another solution to getting testimonials is the user group. In a user group, people share information and ideas about software, hardware, or applications. Groups share information by mail in the form of a newsletter, or they can even have meetings. The most popular library user group has been the Apple Library User Group. Though it does host meetings at the annual ALA conferences, its main communication is its newsletter, which contains firsthand accounts of software use, including questions and answers from people in the field and ways of contacting others.

All software requires documentation—some explanation as to how it works. Sometimes documentation appears on the screen as the program runs, in the form of help files. This self-documenting technique is not sufficient for most software, however, and printed instructions are required. It is not always possible to evaluate documentation before actually purchasing a software package, since it can be difficult to sample a full working package before purchase.

Sources of Software Information

Information about software is available in many places. The best organized software information is in software directories. These directories come in all shapes and sizes, both online and print. Some are collections of reviews of materials, some carry only manufacturer's information. The most comprehensive online directory is *The Menu*, which also has a corresponding print version. The most comprehensive print directory is the Datapro series of directories. A two-volume set, *Microcomputer Software* contains many thousands of listings of all types. Although excellent descriptions of software exist in these books, they are not evaluations. The set is also very expensive.

Meckler Publishing Corporation produces the *Annual Directory of Software Publishers Catalogs*, a microfiche reproduction of over 2000 vendors' brochures and other materials. As a rule, manufacturers' catalogs are also the least organized, the most hyped, and the most useless source of information. They do usually offer basic information about software, such as RAM requirements, disk needs, price, and so on. They may also give brief synopses of the products. Catalogs at least offer the purchaser a source to learn about what is available; specific programs can then be followed up on.

Reviews of software packages can now be found everywhere. Magazines and journals offer the most recent reviews, in an ongoing, up-to-the-minute fashion. Many offer comparisons of major products. Library journals may review library-specific software. The key to successful use of these sources is to find a few that you can relate to in some way. Popular computer magazines may be good for reading about word-processing programs, for example, but they will never review catalog card programs. They will also very seldom have reviews by librarians. In another example, if you are a public librarian, you may not want to rely on the opinions of a research librarian about catalog card programs.

In general, the longer the review, the more time the reviewer spent analyzing the software. Some journals and magazines also provide screenshots, which are snapshots of the actual working screen of the program. These can provide a quick look at the program's appearance on the screen, especially important in the case of educational programs.

Finally, obtaining a working copy, or at least a demonstration or partially disabled copy, will provide even more insight into the workings of the program. So, too, will the documentation. Occasionally, the purchase of a demonstration copy can later be applied toward the purchase of the full system.

Accounting

Accounting software is often used in libraries for preparing payroll, tracking budget expenditures, or performing many of the other routine tasks necessary to run a library operation. Most of these things can be done with a basic spreadsheet program, but ready-made accounting programs do not require as much set-up time and planning. Some accounting programs are very general; others cover only a specific area such as invoicing, making it possible to select a system that does a very specific task.

Accounting tasks can also be done using many integrated software programs and spreadsheets, both described elsewhere in this volume.

Name:	**Accountant, Inc.**
Program type:	Accounting package
Vendor:	Softsync/BLOC Publishing
Cost:	$299
Hardware requirements:	Macintosh
Description:	A complete accounting package, *Accountant, Inc.* will perform a variety of important tasks. The central module of the system is a double entry bookkeeping system. Entries can be made from invoices, credit memos, purchase orders, and journals. Accounts in the general ledger are automatically debited. Up to 13 different financial periods can be created with corresponding reports and analysis. The year-end closing is also automated. Additional features include: flexible count names, password protection, audit trails, and income statements and balance sheets.
	In addition, it will handle payroll with built-in tax tables. A project management feature will assign employees, bills, or purchased items to a specific project.
	The Macintosh's pull-down menus and ease of use are featured throughout. Data from this program may be exported very easily to word processors, databases, and spreadsheets.
Review sources:	*Macuser*, November 1987, 136
Documentation:	Manual of installation procedures and instructions

Name:	**Attorney's Billable Hours**
Program type:	Billing system
Vendor:	Right On Programs
Cost:	$189
Hardware requirements:	IBM and compatibles, with hard-disk drive
Description:	A simple-to-operate system for maintaining a record of time spent helping clients. Will calculate charges and adjustments, and other information is maintained with charge codes. System is security code protected.
Documentation:	Simple instructions

Name:	**EZ Ledger**
Program type:	Budgeting and acquisitions
Vendor:	Right On Programs
Cost:	$99
Hardware requirements:	Apple II series; IBM and compatibles
Description:	This program can be put to use almost as soon as it is taken from the box. There is no need to set up equations and formulas as with spreadsheets. While the versatility is less than that of generic bookkeeping systems, it is very simple to operate and requires no extensive learning or set-up time. Once accounts have been created, users are ready to begin. All budgeted items may be maintained and tracked using budget codes. Main menu functions permit: making a new code; deleting or editing a code; changing code numbers; entering, editing, and deleting data; printing the ledger; making a new data disk; and switching data disks. Entered items are assigned by code and deducted from the budget. Actual cost of an item may be changed or entered upon receipt, if desired. *EZ Ledger* is not a complete ordering or acquisitions program, but it will serve the needs of many small libraries that need to track materials and maintain a budget throughout the year.
Documentation:	Simple instructions

Name:	**Invoicing Control**
Program type:	Invoice and statement generation
Vendor:	Right On Programs
Cost:	$99
Hardware requirements:	IBM and compatibles
Description:	This system will produce invoices and statements from user-supplied data. Documents, which can be printed on any computer paper will contain the library's name, address, phone, and message. The program will also print and total

all outstanding orders at any time to screen or paper. Items may be coded to allow for easy entry of subsequent orders. Extremely easy to learn and use, it can be used for overdues in a small library.

Documentation: Simple instructions

Name: **OfficeWorks**
Program type: *AppleWorks* and *Microsoft Works* template accessory
Vendor: K–12 MicroMedia
Cost: $49.95
Hardware requirements: Apple II series; IBM and compatibles
Description: This template set for general office use can be easily modified, or used as is, for many types of library work. As with other template sets, this one is easy to use. Forms for spreadsheets and word processing components are copied into the computer for immediate use. They include: accounts payable ledger, accounts payable schedule, accounts receivable ledger, accounts receivable schedule, balance sheet, bank reconciliation, budget report, calendar, cash receipts journal, check register, daily reminder, expanded check register, general ledger, income statement, inventory, invoice, payroll register, petty cash register, purchase order, purchase requisition, and statement of account.
Related programs: *AppleWorks* or *Microsoft Works*
Documentation: Manual of simple instructions and descriptions of templates

Name: **PC Accountant**
Program type: Accounting package
Vendor: PC Accountant
Cost: $295
Hardware requirements: IBM and compatibles
Description: A full accounting package with modules for general ledger, accounts receivable, accounts payable, inventory, sales and invoicing, multistate payroll, purchase orders, return merchandise authorizations, job cost, billing materials, fixed assets and depreciation, password security, and custom reports and labels. Powerful system allows for unlimited file size (available disk space is the only limit). Will permit import of database files created by popular databases or export of files in several formats
Documentation: Installation instructions and operation description

Acquisitions

The acquisition software described in this section can assist a library in automating its acquisition of materials. Like everything else, acquisitions may be accomplished in more than one way. Just how a particular library should go about it depends largely upon the type of library, the available computer resources (both skill and hardware), and what the library intends to accomplish.

Some libraries have only the simplest acquisitions needs, such as maintenance of an order file with basic order data (price, order date, call number, etc.). Larger libraries with bigger budgets usually need to track their ordered materials, beginning with the request being put into the system and ending with the material being received by the library—through the generation of regular reports of encumbered and expended funds, ordered price versus actual price, to which department the material should go after it has been received, etc. These functions go far beyond the generation of a simple order list.

The two basic forms of acquisitions software are do-it-yourself and off-the-shelf programs. Neither type is necessarily easier, nor does either imply a lack of sophistication. Both contain programs that are flexible to some degree. Certainly, either may also be expensive, costing as much as $1000 or more.

Do-it-yourself programs are not specifically geared to library needs. They were created for the much wider business or personal computer market. These programs include *dBase* and *AppleWorks*, as well as others. They are described elsewhere in this book. *AppleWorks* is simple enough to use, especially for the generation of an order file. This program is an excellent choice for a small library with minimum needs, especially if it already owns an Apple II series computer.

Off-the-shelf programs—designed for a specific purpose, with no user programming required—include *Acquisitions Control, ETTACQ,* and *Bib-Base/Acq.* These programs are described in this section. Such stand-alone systems as hardware and software combinations, such as the *BetaPhone,* are also off-the-shelf programs.

Of primary importance in selecting software for acquisitions is determining the level of sophistication needed. A list of needs can most often be compiled after brainstorming sessions with the acquisitions staff. Simple narratives from the staff of the present work process are also a sound basis for assessing needs. It is also necessary to actually examine the various software packages, to improve the current system, not just to automate it.

Small libraries, after needs assessment, might find these described programs helpful: *Acquisitions Control, BetaPhone,* and *BT Link.* Medium-sized libraries' needs may be better met by *ETTACQ* or *MATSS*; large libraries might consider *Bib-Base/Acq* or *dBase* (or other relational database system), described later in this book.

Some typical acquisitions tasks that acquisitions software might be used for follow.

Ordering list for books, periodicals, and continuations
Checking for duplicates
Generating order slips or letters
Fund accounting
Coding (e.g., type of media)
Claiming materials not received
Accumulating orders for batch ordering
Producing statistical ordering data (who orders how many books, etc.)
Maintaining encumbered and expended files
Checking new books in on arrival
Creating bibliographies of new books
Integrating other programs (e.g., catalog card production)
Boolean searching

Name:	**Accession Control**
Program type:	Accession control
Vendor:	Right On Programs
Cost:	$99
Hardware requirements:	IBM and compatibles
Description:	For the small or medium-sized library, this program allows users to track their purchases. Menu permits entry or edit of listings, and search. These tasks may be performed by title, author, number or date. ''Wild cards'' or upper and lower case may be used to increase search accuracy. A search result may be sent to the screen or printer. Books may also be searched by a specific date of acquisition, making it possible to create lists of new titles for distribution. Totaling books and cost by month, period, or year is also possible. The program will accept any user-defined accession number up to eight digits. Accession numbers may be reused. Books may be coded to show that they are no longer available.

Printer settings and switching data disks are also under menu control and are easy to perform.

Documentation: Simple set of instructions

Name: **Acquisitions Control**
Program type: Acquisitions
Vendor: Right On Programs
Cost: $129
Hardware requirements: IBM and compatibles; Apple II series
Description: The system allows entry of orders with accompanying encumbering of funds to various accounts. Account totals are constantly updated, as with a spreadsheet. Shipping, handling, discounts, and even tax may be included during process. Menu selections provide good, yet simple control over the process. Orders may be added, deleted, edited, or entered. Coded system facilitates recall of vendors; each need be entered only once. Order forms allow for input of author, publisher, place, year, series, number of copies, edition, volume, ISBN, etc. Orders may be searched, displayed, or printed out. Small libraries with limited needs can look to this as a possible selection for book purchase tracking. Continuous, multi-copy order forms available.
Documentation: Simple set of instructions

Name: **BetaPhone**
Program type: Online ordering system
Vendor: Baker and Taylor
Cost: $350 per year rental
Hardware requirements: Baker and Taylor supplied BetaPhone, a small handheld computer unit with built-in software. No other accessories required.
Description: The system provides for entering ISBN numbers, storing them, and then sending them as a batch to Baker and Taylor over the phone. The small unit is extremely easy to use. It uses a modem coupled to any telephone to transmit orders. In just a few days, order slips arrive in the mail, saving the trouble and bother of much typing. A limited but very effective system. The Maywood (Ill.) Public Library has been using this system for about five years. It has served the library's needs very well.
Documentation: Foolproof instructions

Name: **Bib-Base/Acq**
Program type: Acquisitions and bibliographic production

Vendor: Small Library Computing, Inc.

Cost: $895; $45 demonstration package with manual—cost may be applied towards full purchase later.

Hardware requirements: IBM and compatibles, with hard-disk drive

Description: *Bib-Base/Acq* is a spectacular full-fledged system for tracking acquisitions from start to finish. It produces reports at any point and provides statistical data. It also uses MARC-tagged fields for libraries that require them. It is also integrated—part of a family of software programs (by the same company) that work together, forming a sophisticated overall software environment. This program is expensive (at least when compared with some of the low-cost products in this category), but it is user friendly and menu driven. It works only with an IBM or compatible computer. This program is the acquisitions module of a bibliographic database. It is totally menu driven and, for such a sophisticated system, very easy to operate. Its bibliographic functions allow variable length data fields and records. Records are indexed by author, title, ISBN, call number, and accession number. There are two types of fields: fixed (predefined) and bibliographic. Fixed fields include dates, price, format, etc. Bibliographic fields are entered by using system's full-screen text editor with wraparound.

The system also keeps tabs on encumbered and expended funds, and prints order slips and purchase orders. Items may be tracked from the point at which they are ordered to the final cataloging process. Lists of unfilled, filled, or other types of orders may be printed on demand. Budgeted amounts may be assigned to each fund, type, and supplier. The system keeps track of totals after expenditures and encumbered amounts have been entered.

The select, sort, and list functions allow for reports of almost any type, in numerical order by accession number, by call number (if material has been cataloged), by materials not yet received, by date, etc. *Bib-Base/Marc,* an optional module, will load and use full MARC-format records and output MARC-format records for transfer to other systems. Reports may be printed on 3 × 5 cards (not catalog cards) or in a variety of other ways by telling the program how the page should be formatted: offset printed form, determine page headings, and set number of lines per page.

Files are limited only by disk storage capacity (the database has room for up to 2 billion characters). Two hundred suppliers may be entered; 200 different funds may be defined; 54 record status codes may be defined; 200 other special codes or "types" may be used for further tracking of expenditures and ordering. The system limits are 1000 records on 360K disk drives and 3500 records on 1.2 megabyte (high-density AT) drives. The limits will vary according to size of records entered (e.g., more short than long records will fit on a disk).

This excellent system is highly sophisticated and flexible, but may represent overkill for many small or medium-sized libraries. The system also takes time to learn to operate, especially if MARC-tagged fields are employed. In any case, its big price tag makes it prohibitive for very small and budget-conscious libraries.

Related programs: *Bib-Base/Marc*

Documentation: More than 150 pages in a manual describe the system in detail, with step-by-step instructions and explanations. Appendix A tells how to handle error messages (start-up errors, operating errors, and indexing errors). Appendix B tells how to create multiple databases (e.g., it is possible to create separate databases of titles received in previous years). Appendix D describes order output formats and gives examples of 3 × 5 cards. Several types of forms may be automatically generated, including order form, backup copy format, actual order form format, order summary form, and purchase order output option. Formats may be sent to disk instead of paper. Appendix Z is a summary of all MARC tags acceptable to *Bib-Base*.

Name: **BT Link**

Program type: Online ordering system

Vendor: Baker and Taylor

Cost: Module I Ordering is free; Module II Database, annual subscription of $695; Module III Inventory, annual subscription of $300.

Hardware requirements: IBM and compatibles, Hayes-compatible modem

Description: This electronic acquisitions system allows users to have full control over their order list prior to transmittal by modem. Orders may be checked for duplicates. Provided with the system is a database on CD-ROM, which contains 1.2 million titles of materials of all types. Once orders have been identified on CD-ROM, they can be ordered through Baker and Taylor using the Ordering module. The Inventory module tells how many items are in stock at the Baker and Taylor warehouse.

Name:	**ETTACQ**
Program type:	Acquisitions
Vendor:	Tellingware
Cost:	$900
Hardware requirements:	Apple II series; Macintosh; IBM and compatibles
Description:	This package was developed by a programmer who also worked in a library and continued to work closely with staff in its development. It accommodates 32,000 orders per year (books, continuations, or periodicals). Completely menu-driven package is exceptionally easy to use. It is much easier to learn to use than the more sophisticated *Bib-Base/Acq*. Some of the features include order slip generation on continuous feed paper, checking for duplicate orders by author and title, and printing claim and cancellation notices for overdue orders. Orders may be typed in a batch, corrected, and then printed on special continuous order forms. Reports include on order, on claim, in process, monthly reports of standing orders, serial and periodical orders to be placed, and more.

Vendor file will support 30 vendors, with amount of money encumbered with each, amount spent, number of titles and volumes ordered and received, average number of days to fill order, and average discount percentage. Changes in credit and debit of vendor records are easy to make, and vendor information may be recalled or printed out at any time—and updated with each new entry. Selector file will hold 30 selectors, with amount of money encumbered or spent, number of titles or volumes selected, and the same credit and debit ability for any field (or view or print selector information). All three files are updated with each entry.

Orders may be placed with the following fields: title, author, ISBN, publisher, call number, vendor, four funds and four selectors per order, date ordered, reference number (defined by user), and notes. Orders may also be downloaded from an outside optical disk source or maintained in consideration file. Users may enter up to 200 orders at one sitting, with up to 7000 orders on the disk at one time.

Fund accounting will analyze library expenditures by subject area and selector fund areas.

Documentation:	Excellent tutorial and user manual is an easy-to-follow, walk-through, looseleaf notebook

Name:	**ETTSEL**
Program type:	Automated selection system
Vendor:	Tellingware
Cost:	$150; annual support, $50 (six month free support); site license, $50
Hardware requirements:	IBM and compatibles
Description:	Automated selection process provides libraries with priority purchasing options. Librarians read reviews of interest, then enter bibliographic information and priority code of 0 to 9. At appropriate time, materials are then ordered based on amount of money available and the priority codes. Subject areas may also be prioritized and the highest cost acceptable for an item may also be entered. The final list may be edited and unwanted items removed. It is then printed out as a list or as purchase orders, or it sends purchase orders electronically to *ETTACQ*, an automated acquisitions system (available separately and discussed above).

Each librarian may have his or her own system and maintain data on a separate floppy disk. Up to 100 subjects and 100 categories of selection may be defined. Once fields are defined, materials may be entered into the database. Items are checked for duplication by title and ISBN.

The system will accommodate up to 600 selections per disk (IBM) or 350 selections per disk (Apple II). Fields that are available for use are title, author, ISBN, call number, reference number, publisher and edition, series, notes, cost, number of volumes, purchase priority, category, five subjects, journal, and media type. Search may be by title, author, series, category, or subject.

The system will produce custom multi-part forms for use with ordering. Orders can in some cases be sent electronically to library vendor.

Related programs:	*ETTACQ*
Documentation:	Excellent manual with instructions for installation and use

Name:	**MATSS** (Midwest Automated Technical Services Software)
Program type:	Acquisitions
Vendor:	Midwest Library Service
Cost:	$4,294 for full system. Acquisitions system includes all related Technical Services modules (below), as well as 12 hours of on-site training, manuals, order production, vendor reporting, open order database access, fund accounting, and automatic claiming and cancellation. Electronic transmis-

sion of orders, and label and spine label production are also included. Annual maintenance, $300 (includes toll-free telephone support and software releases and updates). Training is available at $250 per day.

Demonstration package: $50 (applicable to purchase price).

Hardware requirements: IBM and compatibles, with hard-disk drive; Hayes-compatible modem

Description: This complete acquisitions system performs fund accounting, catalog card data entry and production, spine and label production, and order form production. It also serves as communications program for downloading MARC records from online utilities for use with any of program's other functions. Original records (manual entry) may be produced with order and catalog entry program, which includes sophisticated text editor.

The accounting program takes its data directly as orders are placed, and keeps encumbered accounts up to date. Funds may later be unencumbered at the original price and expended at actual price.

Perhaps the program's most striking aspect is its ease of use. The main menu offers quick and easy movement to any program activity. Other features are password protection and extensive ability to customize. This new version of program now supports Library of Congress in two formats, Dewey and National Library of Medicine call numbers, bill-to/ship-to address, reports displayed to screen or printed out, and duplicate order checking.

Vendor information may be searched by name, number, or fiscal year. The program includes quantities and dollar amounts of items on order, filled, and cancelled; prints mailing labels; generates purchase orders by author/title or title/author sequence; supports Standard Access Number (SAN); and is capable of electronic transmission of orders to any vendor that accepts BISAC variable record format. Fund accounting supports multiple fiscal years and has three levels for report subtotaling. Summary records keep track of each fund, and special report indicates accounts above or below chosen percentage in expense encumbered or available balance.

Purchase orders are numbered automatically; vendor, purchase order number, copies, fund accounts, and comments may be defaulted. There is a full-screen editor. Reorders may be produced from open order file without rekeying, and multiple batches of orders may be processed at one time.

The open order database can be searched by author, title, LCCN, ISBN, or a unique record number. Scrolling a summary of all MARC tags recognized by MATSS is possible.

The system will handle a total of 32,500 vendors, 32,500 accounts, and 32,500 records in open order file.

Documentation: Large volume of information containing complete data on setup and use

Name: **Nonesuch Acquisitions System**

Program type: Acquisitions

Vendor: Ringgold Management Systems, Inc.

Cost: $2,500 per terminal

Hardware requirements: IBM and compatibles, with hard-disk drive

Description: This full-system acquisitions system provides fund accounting and electronic ordering. It does not provide possible related modes such as ILL, serial management, or an online catalog.

Bibliography

Librarians have been producing lists of materials for as long as there have been libraries. The bibliography generator is one of the easiest to understand and use forms of library-related software as well as one of the most popular. Some libraries need only "quick bibs," which consist of little more than the barest data—not even in a rigorously standardized format, save that it is internally consistent. Other libraries require full bibliographies in a highly standardized format, including annotations.

It is perfectly possible and acceptable to use a word processor and even a database management system to create bibliographies. A program such as *Bibliography Writer* is designed specifically for this purpose, however, and will ensure that all entries will be consistent.

Name:	**Bib/Rite Bibliography Writer**
Program type:	Bibliography production
Vendor:	Robert E. Litke
Cost:	$45.95, one computer, one user; $150, one computer, multiple users; $24.95, additional styles
Hardware requirements:	IBM and compatibles; Apple II series
Description:	Among the many features is one good timesaver called a macro—by just pressing a single key, the user may input a full journal title that is used regularly. Entries may be added or deleted. Full citations may be moved, replaced, inserted, or have characters deleted. Entries may be sorted alphabetically by author or into subcategories by author. A finished bibliography will be printed with automatic margins, headings, and page numbers. Citations will not break between pages. Bibliographic styles are available for the American Psychological Association, Modern Language Association, and American Medical Association. Capacity is approximately 150 in Apple II with 64K of memory and 361 in an IBM or compatibles (the actual number may be larger,

depending on the memory of the computer in use). Excellent, high quality program offering a range of styles and options.

Review sources: *ASHA*, May 1985, 73.

"This Teacher's Pet," *Computer Shopper*, October 1984, 368.

"Bib/Rite Gets 'B' in Bibliography," *Computer Shopper*, October 1984, 94.

Documentation: Very good 37-page manual. Contains complete installation instructions, a quick tour, data entry suggestions, and style considerations.

Name: **Bibliography Generator**

Program type: Bibliography production

Vendor: Educational Activities, Inc.

Cost: $59.95 (includes backup)

Hardware requirements: IBM and compatibles

Description: This program is licensed by the Modern Language Association and uses their style to create bibliographies. Easy to use, the program will handle magazine articles, books, and other media. The program automatically capitalizes, uses colons correctly, underlines, etc. Users may customize each bib by selecting the margins, page length, spacing between lines, and whether to number pages. Printing may vary by entire bibliography, one heading, or a single citation. A file may even be transferred to a word processor. Entries may be saved for future editing and given headings and subheadings. A help option gives support during use. Compatible with all printers. Help option available throughout.

Documentation: Notebook containing instructions, examples

Name: **Bibliography Maker**

Program type: Bibliography production

Vendor: Right On Programs

Cost: $99

Hardware requirements: IBM and compatibles

Description: This program uses the Modern Language Association for a guide for preparing bibliographies. It is suitable for creating term paper bibliographies and reading lists for distribution to patrons. Data is easily entered for each item, sorted and printed as needed. Bibliographies may be saved for later use and editing. Search function permits easy retrieval of single items.

Documentation: Simple, easy-to-follow

Name: **Bibliography Writer**
Program type: Bibliography production
Vendor: Follett Software Company
Cost: $59.95
Hardware requirements: Apple II series
Description: Simple, straightforward program allowing for bibliography title (30 characters) and up to 300 entries (150 if annotations are included). Users decide which items are to be included, and the input screen is customized accordingly. Items may include only author and title. More extensive entries may also include call number, place of publication, publisher, copyright date and annotation. Printing may be by author, title, or call number order. Space is limited by number of disks only.
Documentation: Simple booklet

Name: **List Maker**
Program type: Bibliography production
Vendor: Right On Programs
Cost: $85
Hardware requirements: IBM and compatibles; Apple II series
Description: Extremely simple-to-use program. Data is entered from main menu for a list of any type. Program specializes in name and address files. Work begins with a Master List. All data goes into this file. As necessary, sublists are created by pulling them from the Master List. Individual lists may be created or deleted as desired. Labels can also be produced.
Documentation: Simple booklet

Name: **Subject List**
Program type: Bibliography production
Vendor: Right On Programs
Cost: $85
Hardware requirements: IBM and compatibles; Apple II series
Description: Bibliography program provides for easy way to create new acquisitions list. Once data entry is complete a printout can be made by author, title, or subject. All fields can be searched. Bibliographies can be saved, and books can be entered or deleted easily.
Documentation: Simple booklet

Catalog Cards

Catalog card production on a microcomputer is popular. Many packages are similar, but purchasers should be aware of significant differences in cataloging rules, the ease with which entries may be corrected, whether cards may be stored for batch printing later, whether there is onscreen review of material exactly as it will be printed out (before it is printed), and whether a system will produce spine and book pocket labels.

A major problem in generating cards with a microcomputer is the fanfold catalog card paper. Most printers will not take thick card stock or paper that has "microfine" perforations (i.e., perforations which, after separation, produce cards identical to regular 3 × 5 cards). Special bottom-feed printers are available that handle card stock with no difficulty.

Name:	**Avant Cards**
Program type:	Catalog Card Production
Vendor:	Addison (Ill.) Public Library
Cost:	$250 per license package (disks, support, documentation)
Hardware requirements:	Apple II series; IBM and compatibles
Description:	An excellent catalog card production system, perhaps the most sophisticated available. Written by a technical services librarian. Clear and complete instructions are provided for creating working disks and installing the program on a hard disk. Some of its many features included full control over card and label formats, minimal keystrokes for usual cases, label printing, batch printing, 12 call number and shelving information fields, proof printing of data, *AACR2* punctuation, and up to eight subject headings and eight added entries at a time.
Review sources:	*Library Software Review*, July–August, 1989, 221.
Documentation:	Loose-leaf binder, 100 pages, indexed. Contains installation instructions, and clear and illustrated methods for achieving good results. One of the best documented catalog card pro-

grams to be found. Also comes with troubleshooting manual.

Name:	**C.A.L.M. (Card and Label Manager)**
Program type:	Catalog card and label production
Vendor:	Speak Softly, Inc.
Cost:	$169
Hardware requirements:	Apple II series; IBM and compatibles
Description:	System will produce catalog cards and pocket, spine, and card labels. Has been under improvement for many versions. Features include support of Dewey and LC cataloging, ability to print from menu in three sizes with dot matrix printer, as many tracings as desired, and three label formats. System has a lot of power, allowing the production of up to seven continuation cards, cataloging of all types of materials, and full text editing.

Name:	**Cassy**
Program type:	Catalog card production
Vendor:	Diakon Systems
Cost:	$20 (shareware)
Hardware requirements:	IBM and compatibles
Description:	Menu-driven system produces catalog cards and shelf list cards. Cards are printed in the order that makes filing easier. The number of fields available for books are: accession date (6), author (25), title (70), call letters (3), publisher (15), copyright date (6), source (10), cost (9), remarks (32), classification number (10) and up to five subject headings (40 each).
Review sources:	*Library Software Review*, July–August, 1989, 221.

Name:	**Catalog Card and Label Writer**
Program type:	Catalog card production
Vendor:	K–12 MicroMedia
Cost:	$169
Hardware requirements:	Apple II series; IBM and compatibles. Can be installed on a hard drive.
Description:	Completed information can be saved to disk for use with *AppleWorks* to produce, for example, accession lists. Information for each entry is entered and edited a complete screen at a time. Formatted card can be previewed prior to printing. Will print spine and book pocket labels as well as catalog cards. Uses *AACR2*, or can be changed as desired.

Completed cards can be printed as a batch, and as many copies as required can be printed.

Documentation: Short notebook with examples and guidelines

Name: **Catalog Carder**
Program type: Catalog card production
Vendor: Right On Programs
Cost: $99; continuous feed catalog cards are also available for $30 for 1000
Hardware requirements: IBM and compatibles; Apple II series
Description: Menu-driven program is easy to use. It produces quality catalog cards with *AACR2* catalog format using onscreen prompts and onscreen editing and previewing. Data for 25 cards may be entered and then printed out as a batch to save time. Some custom production of card format is permitted. Card set consists of two author cards, title card, up to four subject cards, editor/joint author/illustrator card, additional copies of any or all cards, and complete tracings. Cards may be printed separately, as needed.
Documentation: Simple booklet

Name: **Catalog Carder—AV**
Program type: Catalog card production
Vendor: Right On Programs
Cost: $99
Hardware requirements: IBM and compatibles; Apple II series
Description: This program is essentially like *Catalog Carder*, described earlier. It is geared to audiovisual materials, such as filmstrips, computer software, films, records, videocassettes, etc. Totally menu controlled, it permits the retrieval of a specific card, or the printing of only an author card, title card, subject card, joint author card, illustrator card, or a shelf list card. A complete set may also be printed out for a single entry or for all entries that are currently in the database.
Documentation: Small booklet

Name: **Librarian's Helper: Productivity Tool for Librarians**
Program type: Catalog card production
Vendor: Scarecrow Press
Cost: IBM and compatibles: free demonstration package; $250, enhanced version; $175, basic system. Apple: no demon-

stration package available; $350, enhanced version, including CP/M card; $175, user-supplied CP/M card.

Hardware requirements: Apple II series (with CP/M card); IBM and compatibles

Description: Excellent and easy-to-use program provides exceptional quality for the production of catalog cards. Complete package provides for multiple card sets, onscreen viewing, and saving material to disk for bibliography or database production, all according to *AACR2* cataloging rules. Any of the available 32 data fields may be eliminated from the data entry routine if they are not needed. Program is menu-driven; information is fed in at prompts. Program provides easy editing of records at any point. Custom configuration available if proper information is given to Scarecrow Press when order is placed. Special "save" feature, available for additional charge, permits records to be saved to disk for later printing, and to print out information as a bibliography sorted by author, title, or call number. Data may even be transferred from disk to online catalogs and database programs. Several new features include "backup," which allows editing previous entries; diagnostic and repair program which will recover damaged files; data security routine; and improved sort time.

Review sources: *Library Software Review*, March–April, 1991, 144.

Documentation: Excellent manual, containing instructions, setup, etc.

Name: **LPS Catalog Card Program**

Program type: Catalog card production (label production program under development)

Vendor: G-N-G Software

Cost: $200; label production program to cost $50

Hardware requirements: Apple II series

Description: Excellent and easy-to-use program for creating catalog cards. Records are stored on disk for later processing. User may create full or individual sets of catalog cards (shelflist, author, title, one to five subjects, series), and book lists for inventory, subject lists, and new books. System will add or delete entries, sort numerically by call number, and allow for Dewey, LC, or local cataloging of up to ten-place Cutter numbers. Permits subject search by key word or groups of call numbers in tracing or anywhere on card. Books can be designated as easy, professional, reference, or paperback.

Documentation: Good notebook of instructions, illustrations, and setup guide

Name: **LPS Catalog Card—Spine/Pocket/Labels Program**

Program type: Catalog card production

Vendor: G-N-G Software

Cost: $250

Hardware requirements: IBM and compatibles

Description: Program provides all features of the main system listed above, plus label production. Labels include: type of publication, classification number, author letters or Cutter number, and volume or copy number. Pocket and card labels also carry author, title, and biographee, for biographies. Will utilize data produced and stored in catalog card program. Labels printed in all caps. Requires official OCLC continuous pin-fed, pressure sensitive labels.

Documentation: Notebook filled with examples of catalog cards, instructions.

Name: **MacCards**

Program type: Catalog card production

Vendor: Caspr

Cost: $269, full system; $25, demonstration package (can be used as credit towards full system). The demonstration package is exactly the same as the full system except that the print function has been disabled.

Hardware requirements: Macintosh

Description: Very user-friendly catalog card production system. Using the mouse and icons, librarian can quickly begin producing catalog cards. Full screen editing shows the field titles in a column on the right; data is filled in on the left. Has the additional advantage of cut-and-paste of text from one field to another. Data is used to produce catalog cards as well as to create a database of bibliographic records for later use. Fields are: catalog number, author, author statement, place of publication, date, pagination and series, notes, local accession number, LCCN, tracings (20 subject headings and 9 added entries), title, subtitle, edition, publisher, price, source, location, and ISBN. Each file may contain up to 1500 records with variable length fields and up to 512 characters per record. Cards may be printed according to *AACR2* or with local punctuation. Program will print card set or multiple set, main entry card, author and title added entry cards, subject cards, and a shelf list card. Title and main entry cards have a hanging indentation. Also supports label printing, test printing, a single label for current record, and multiple label production.

Documentation: Booklet, 33 pages, includes index, screenshots, and explanations and examples of each function.

Name: **Quick Card**
Program type: Catalog card production
Vendor: Follett Software Company
Cost: $234.95, IBM; $159.95, Apple
Hardware requirements: IBM and compatibles; Apple II series
Description: Once data has been entered for a catalog card, the user can go back and make whatever changes or corrections are required. The system will produce catalog cards and book and spine labels. Fields are call number (64 characters), author (80 characters), title (150 characters), responsibility area (80 characters), edition area (80 characters), note area (240 characters), analytics (6 fields of 76 characters), ISBN number (80 characters), subject headings (6 fields of 76 characters), added entries (6 fields of 76 characters), accession number (12 characters), vendor area (48 characters), and requestor (3 fields of 76 characters). Although the program is not as versatile and cannot be custom formatted to the extent of a program such as *Librarian's Helper*, it is extremely easy to use. It will print arabic and roman numerals in the tracings. A second card is printed if the data will not entirely fit on the first. Dewey or LC numbers are allowed. Uses *AACR2* rules. Will automatically format for hanging indentations for title and main entry cards. The program can print multiple sets of cards and labels, a single card, a range of cards, or proofsheets for editing.
Review sources: *The Computing Teacher*, November 1985, 49.
Related programs: Compatible with *Circulation Plus*.
Documentation: Excellent manual with sample cards

Name: **Rachels Catalog Card Printer**
Program type: Catalog card production
Vendor: Rachels, Peter Konnecker
Cost: Shareware registration fee: $25, Apple II; $29, IBM; $39, Macintosh. Trial copies available for $4, $5, and $6, respectively.
Hardware requirements: Macintosh; Apple II series; IBM and compatibles
Description: This high-value shareware program is extremely easy to set up and use. System will print individual cards, sets of cards,

labels and book lists. *AACR2* punctuation is used. Additional features include two added entries and four subjects. Once data has been entered into the form, it may be printed out on paper or saved to disk and printed as part of a batch later. Approximately 100 cards (32K per file) may be saved in a particular file.

Cards may also be previewed easily. In the Macintosh version, clicking the preview selection will give a graphic representation of how the printed card will look.

This program is extremely impressive and capable. Small libraries especially should investigate its purchase. It may be shared among libraries without cost for previewing. Only a registration fee is necessary if the library decides to continue using it.

Review sources: *Apple Library Users Group Newsletter*, April 1989.
Documentation: Short manual of 24 pages amply describes system with instructions, screenshots, and tutorial.

Name: **Riley's Catalog Cards**
Program type: Catalog card production
Vendor: Richard K. Riley
Cost: $45 (shareware)
Hardware requirements: IBM and compatibles
Description: Excellent and easy-to-use program for creating catalog cards. First-time users can begin producing catalog cards within minutes. Menu driven, user friendly. Uses standard *AACR2* format.
Documentation: Self-documenting

Name: **RLibrary/Cards**
Program type: Catalog card production
Vendor: Rachels, Peter Konnecker
Cost: $139; demonstration disk available for $5
Hardware requirements: Macintosh
Description: Easy-to-use catalog card workstation. Macintosh windows provide quick and convenient access to the program. Point and click with the mouse and a card can be produced very quickly. Audiovisual cataloging, with a general material description, five-line call number, four formattable notes paragraphs, standard numbers, and up to ten entries are supported. The mouse makes it easy to point and click stock phrases into card. Cataloging help files are available online.

Fully formatted cards can be previewed on screen before printing. Learning time is very short.

Review sources: *Apple Library User Group Newsletter*, January 1990, 77.

Related programs: *RLibrary/LaserCards*

Documentation: Outstanding user manual contains thorough details on setting user options, printing setup and problems, card formatting, various cataloging tasks, shortcuts, printer forms, error messages, etc.

Name: **RLibrary/LaserCards**

Program type: Catalog card production

Vendor: Rachels, Lloyd Konnecker

Cost: $269

Hardware requirements: Macintosh

Description: Similar to *RLibrary/Cards*, but adds style and print features. Will work on a networked or shared printer, an especially useful feature if only one expensive laser printer is available for several machines. Makes use of the Macintosh extended character set, including accents and foreign alphabets. Text styles, including fonts, size and style, can be altered. Program will print up to four continuation cards and allows for print quality choice of draft, faster, or best on some printers. Spool printing is also supported.

Documentation: Thorough and indepth users manual. Detailed information about printers, printing basics, pin-fed printers, sheet-fed printers, fonts and extended character sets, layout, design basics, styles for cards and labels, and troubleshooting. Index.

Catalogs

All libraries need adequate access to their collections. The best access is through a catalog of some type. In the past, catalogs were either a card catalog or a bound volume catalog. The automation of catalogs, especially for smaller or medium-size libraries, is a very welcome occurrence. Libraries can now prepare electronic catalogs of special collections, such as audiovisual collections, book and other printed materials collections, and just about anything else.

Name:	**A-V Catalog Writer**
Program type:	Printed AV catalog
Vendor:	Follett Software Company
Cost:	$79.95
Hardware requirements:	Apple II series
Description:	This easy-to-use program gives the library the ability to create a printed AV catalog for use by patrons, staff, or faculty. The catalog can include films, videotapes, filmstrips, etc. The program may be tailored with media abbreviations that the librarian creates. Preset subject categories may be used, or up to 40 categories may be created to accommodate the library's needs, those which students and other users are most likely to think of when using the system. When complete, each item can be accessed in the catalog by media type, shelflist number, title, producer, contents, copyright date, and up to three subjects. Catalogs can be printed in their entirety or as subsets (e.g., history).
Documentation:	Simple, easy to use, and clearly written booklet

Name:	**Catalog Plus**
Program type:	Online public access catalog
Vendor:	Follett Software Company
Cost:	$1,495
Hardware requirements:	IBM and compatibles, with hard-disk drive

Description: This is an exceptionally good program for those libraries that already use *Circulation Plus*, since data can be moved between programs. Users can find materials in the collection by using Boolean terms, title, author, call number, subject, and ISBN/LCCN, as well as through key word searching in the title, author, note, and subject fields. The catalog will also reveal whether an item is on the shelf or checked out. *Catalog Plus* will read MARC records and can write this data out to floppy disks, if desired. It will also generate records for use with *Quick Card*, a Follett catalog card production system. Both brief and full bibliographic reports can be created as necessary.

Related programs: May be integrated with *Plus Link*, a Follett networking system, and *Circulation Plus*, also Follett.

Documentation: Good manual for startup and reference

Name: **Compulog II**

Program type: Online catalog system

Vendor: Embar Information Consultants, Inc.

Cost: Contact vendor for current pricing

Hardware requirements: IBM and compatibles, with hard-disk drive

Description: Easy-to-use online catalog. Simple startup procedure is followed by data entry into blank forms, or data may be downloaded from OCLC or CD-ROM databases.

From the main menu it is easy to add catalog records. Reports that can be generated include author, subject, title, publisher, shelflist, ISBN list, author authority, subject authority, and source authority. Online search can be in menu-assisted mode or expert mode, with Boolean operators.

This system is of particular interest to small special libraries with limited collections, such as folders of slides, photographs, and architectural drawings.

Related programs: *Compucirc, Compulog-Media*

Name: **Compulog-Media**

Program type: Online catalog system

Vendor: Embar Information Consultants, Inc.

Cost: Contact vendor for current pricing

Hardware requirements: IBM and compatibles, with hard-disk drive

Description: This system is specifically geared to provide an online catalog for media centers and libraries with special collections. Data records can be entered manually using a preset form. From the main menu it is easy to add catalog records.

Reports that can be generated in print or to screen include: LC call number, subject, title, publisher, shelflist, LC call number authority, subject authority, source authority, on-line search, and series list. The catalog may be searched using Boolean operators and keywords.

System is currently in use at the Bronx Community College Learning Center to organize an extensive collection of AV and microcomputer software cataloged by LC and OCLC cards over the past several years.

Name:	**LaserGuide**
Program type:	CD-ROM patron catalog
Vendor:	General Research Corporation
Cost:	Contact vendor for current pricing
Hardware requirements:	IBM and compatibles, with CD-ROM drive
Description:	This patron access catalog allows searching by author, title, and subject. A search will reveal a number of "hits" and the patron can scan them. A subject search will match the request against all of the words of the subject headings. Boolean search is supported in an easy-to-use format for patrons. *LaserGuide* will also suggest additional search topics for patrons. A very nice feature is the library map within the system. Floor plans of the library show patrons where a book should actually be. Map can include different floors or branches. A browsing feature allows patrons to see what books are located nearby the book that they are interested in, just as if they were looking on the actual shelf.

Name:	**LaserQuest**
Program type:	CD-ROM cataloging system
Vendor:	General Research Corporation
Cost:	Contact vendor for current pricing
Hardware requirements:	IBM and compatibles
Description:	This database contains the holdings of over 1000 libraries— more than 6 million USMARC and CANMARC records, and over 2 million pre-1968 MARC records. Access to records is primarily by title. These records can be matched against the library's own shelflist and "hits" added to the database or catalog. Saved records can also be used to create catalog cards and labels. The system is window-driven and easy to use. GRC suggests that the productivity rate is 80 to 100 records per hour. Interfaces for linking *LaserQuest* can be loaded for use directly into the following systems: CLSI,

INLEX, DYNIX, VTLS, MultiLis, GEAC, Winnebago, Carlyle, MOLLI, Columbia and CARL.

Related programs: *LaserGuide*

Name: **MacLAP**
Program type: Online patron access catalog
Vendor: Caspr
Cost: Contact vendor for current pricing
Hardware requirements: Macintosh
Description: Program uses Macintosh icons and graphics in a public access catalog. On the screen, users see the closed drawers of a card catalog. When clicked with the mouse, the drawers open, and a search can be made by author, title, and subject. Right or left truncation is possible. Many commands are made by simply clicking on the graphic. A double-click selects the second card of any card set. All information is displayed in *AACR2* format and punctuation. Search results may be downloaded or printed. Catalog records can be short, medium, or long.

Name: **Mitinet/MARC**
Program type: MARC cataloging
Vendor: Information Transform, Inc.
Cost: $795 (U.S.); $995 (Canada); $95 (U.S. demonstration); $150 (Canada demonstration). Demonstration cost may be used for full credit for complete version within 30 days of purchase of demonstration version. $10 shipping.
Hardware requirements: IBM and compatibles; Apple II series, two drives; Macintosh version available soon
Description: Program creates inhouse MARC format cataloging records. Compatible with over 40 automated systems. Very easy to use. Provides lots of onscreen *AACR2* examples and rule number references for staff. Can create USMARC records for many formats, including books, AV, software, maps, serials, archives, and other. Most users can begin work in just an hour or so—no knowledge of MARC tags, subfields, indicators, fixed fields, ISBN, or *AACR2* is required in order to get the program up and running. New versions incorporate still more features: quicker option selection, custom option file, easier installation process, and much more.
Review sources: ''An Expert System For Notice MARC Catalogers,'' *Wilson Library Bulletin*, November 1987, 33.

Related programs:	*Print-A-Bunch*
Documentation:	Excellent binder with setup instructions, examples, and very detailed information

Name:	**Music Cataloger**
Program type:	Catalog
Vendor:	Right On Programs
Cost:	$99
Hardware requirements:	IBM and compatibles; Apple II series
Description:	Very simple and easy-to-use program for doing one thing well: tracking a special music collection. Finished product is a complete printed catalog on 3 × 5 cards. Screen prompts are used to enter data, including author or composer and title. List may be printed alphabetically by author or composer or by title to screen or printer. May be printed with composer or title on top line, depending on library's needs. Includes supply of 3 × 5 cards.
Documentation:	Simple booklet

Name:	**OCLC Cataloging Micro Enhancer**
Program type:	OCLC online enhancement
Vendor:	OCLC
Cost:	Contact vendor for current pricing
Hardware requirements:	M-300 workstation
Description:	Provides an assortment of special capabilities for the OCLC user, including the automation of many telecommunications functions such as online searching, automatic dialup, logon, logoff, etc., for dialup users. Records can also be edited offline to reduce fees.
Review sources:	"Cataloging for Fifty-five Libraries Using Microcomputer Technology," *Library Hi Tech News*, December 1988, 1.

Name:	**On-Line Audio Catalog**
Program type:	AV catalog
Vendor:	Right On Programs
Cost:	$199
Hardware requirements:	IBM and compatibles
Description:	Using this very simple, extremely easy-to-use program, one can catalog records, tapes, and CDs. Entry information contains call or reference number, composer, title, artist, publishing information, copyright date, play information, up to two lines of annotation, and up to 20 keywords. Search is by composer, title, or any keyword or part thereof. ISBN,

accession number, location, and price may also be included in the entry. System will generate a shelflist card. Libraries with no online system may wish to consider electronic access to at least their AV materials.

Documentation: Simple booklet of instructions

Name: **On-Line Catalog**
Program type: Online catalog
Vendor: Right On Programs
Cost: $249
Hardware requirements: IBM and compatibles, with hard-disk drive; Macintosh, with hard-disk drive
Description: For use by a small library or a department's special library. Easy to set up and operate, the system will even use barcodes if requested. System permits as many records as hard disk will allow. Standard reference is 1000 records per megabyte of disk storage. Menu-driven system provides facsimile of traditional catalog card on computer screen. Search for items may be made by title, author, and six subject headings. A printout by subject of search is also easy to request. System will print out shelflist cards with LC number, ISBN, accession number, location, and price. Fields may be left blank or left out.
Related programs: *On-Line Plus*
Documentation: Simple and easy-to-follow set of instructions

Name: **On-Line Plus**
Program type: Online catalog
Vendor: Right On Programs
Cost: $339
Hardware requirements: IBM and compatibles, hard-disk drive; Macintosh, hard-disk drive
Description: Includes features of *On-Line Catalog*, above, plus *Catalog Carder*, a catalog card production system that produces complete sets of catalog cards for entries.
Related programs: *On-Line Catalog, Catalog Carder*
Documentation: Simple and easy-to-follow set of instructions

Name: **Print-A-Bunch**
Program type: Printing utility for *Mitinet/MARC*
Vendor: Information Transform, Inc.
Cost: $95, plus $10 shipping and handling
Hardware requirements: IBM and compatibles

Description: This print utility will search a *Mitinet/MARC* data disk and print in one of three formats: bibcard, directory, or MARC print. It is not necessary to search, load, print, and erase each record individually. Records to be searched may be selected by a range of record numbers, date-range of publication years, date-range of change or revision of records, type of format, or a combination of these criteria. Program will not print catalog cards.

Related programs: *Mitinet/MARC*

Name: **Smartcat**

Program type: Online catalog development tool

Vendor: MecklerSoft

Cost: $59.95

Hardware requirements: IBM and compatibles

Description: Low-cost program is menu driven and provides for the creation of a sophisticated online catalog. Database contains author, title, classification number, and can be sorted by these same fields. Search of keywords field is Boolean supported. Each match can be displayed in short or long form, and can be saved to a disk file. User interface has popup windows.

Documentation: Notebook of examples, startup, and reference

Name: **SuperCAT**

Program type: Cataloging system

Vendor: Gaylord

Cost: $1,500, software license for one workstation; $250, for additional workstations; additional subscription required for CD-ROM databases

Hardware requirements: IBM and compatibles

Description: Provides a complete stand-alone cataloging workstation. User can create original cataloging records or edit existing ones, and can create catalog cards and labels. Some of the specific features: retrieve MARC records from CD-ROM using LCCN, title, author, ISSN/ISBN; save MARC records to local storage for future use; create original cataloging templates; preview formatted cards and labels on screen, prior to printing; print edit sheets for offline review; display MARC tag descriptions during editing; use three printers simultaneously. In addition, the program has a host of utilities and special features: format disks online, generate reports, display help at any time, and define macros on five function keys.

Review sources:	"SuperCAT Cataloger's Workstation," *CD-ROM Librarian*, September 1989, 28.
Documentation:	Extensive binder contains installation and care instructions, cataloging procedures, printing details, and much more. Glossary and index also help. Appended: Troubleshooting; Card and Label Stock; CLSI Link; Export; Local Area Network; and more.
Name:	**TermMARC**
Program type:	Online catalog
Vendor:	Small Library Computing, Inc.
Cost:	$200
Hardware requirements:	IBM and compatibles
Description:	System provides for interface with OCLC. MARC records may be saved to a disk file for use locally. Contact vendor for additional information.

CD-ROM Products

Compact disk–read only memory, or CD-ROM, products became possible with the advent of special very large capacity mass storage. While "write once, read many" (WORM) technology exists for CDs, all of the programs discussed below are read only. The implications of read-only are many, but the most important is that the information stored on the disk cannot be changed—users cannot add to the data on the disk.

A CD-ROM product requires software that must be compatible with your computer, and a CD-ROM disk drive. An amazing number of CD-ROM software packages are available for a relatively modest price. (There are, of course, many CD-ROM products for very large and immodest prices.)

The programs listed below are some of the more popular and more library-oriented packages. Some CD-ROM packages contain hundreds of megabytes of clip art and public domain software. These can be used successfully by staff or the public. A CD-ROM is also among the few types of software that can be circulated without too much fear of damage.

Name:	**CD-CATSS**
Program type:	Cataloging and database management system
Vendor:	Utlas
Cost:	$247 per month
Hardware requirements:	IBM and compatibles, with CD-ROM
Description:	System provides cataloging for over 8 million records on nine disks, which may be purchased in groups of three. A 3-disk MARC collection contains 1.5 million entries. System is updated quarterly. Files come from Utlas users, plus National Library of Canada, Library of Congress Books All, Library of Congress Serials, Library of Congress Visual Materials, Library of Congress Maps, Library of Congress Music, Library of Congress Minimal Level, Library of Congress COBRA, the British Library, the Government Printing Office, and the National Library of Medicine. Database includes records in all languages.

Search of database is by title, author, and keyword, with the use of Boolean operators. Numeric search keys provide access by Government Document Number, Publisher's Number for Music, CODEN, Standard Film Number, Standard Technical Report Number, Standard Recording Number, and Report Number. Browsing is also supported. Full screen editing provides for delete, insert, duplicate, and change data or fields. System will print cards and labels from individual records. Sort order can be defined, as well as card and label types.

Documentation: Notebook contains an introduction to the system and CD-ROM database in general, installing the system, getting started help, detailed search instructions, how to create and review a record, how to communicate with CATSS, system management, troubleshooting, and how to print cards and labels.

Name: **General Periodicals Index**

Program type: CD-ROM database

Vendor: Information Access Company

Cost: Contact vendor for current pricing

Hardware requirements: IBM and compatibles

Description: Database of general periodicals contains 100 titles, including newspapers. Available in both a public library edition (current events, consumer information, arts and entertainment, travel, business, etc.) and an academic library edition (scholarly titles in social science and humanities, general interest, business, and management). A range of periodicals useful for the specific library environment. Many citations are available as full text in *Magazine Collection* and *Business Collection*. Database is updated each month. System is very easy to use with only occasional intervention.

Related programs: *Backfile Subscription*, four years ($2,950)

Documentation: Online user help. Paper documentation also included.

Name: **Grolier Electronic Encyclopedia**

Program type: CD-ROM database

Vendor: Grolier Educational Corporation

Cost: $395

Hardware requirements: IBM and compatibles, with CD-ROM; Macintosh, with CD-ROM

Description: This CD-ROM product is excellent for use by students. It provides not only text but full-color pictures as well. The text is the complete edition of the *Academic American Encyclopedia*, over 33,000 articles. Access to any article or picture is quick, and entries can be searched with a two- or three-word search combination, as well as by truncation. Text may be saved on an IBM disk format or printed out. The system provides a complete warranty and technical service. Teacher's guide and activity sheets help teach research skills in literature, language arts, history, math and science, and reference.

Review sources: *Booklist*, July 1989, 1878.
PC Magazine, January 31, 1989.
The Reading Teacher, February 1991, 432.

Documentation: User's guide

Name: **InfoTrac Backfile Database**
Program type: Magazine index
Vendor: Information Access Company
Cost: $2,950; annual updates, $950
Hardware requirements: System hardware is included in the price, and supplied by the manufacturer
Description: Retrospective data for *InfoTrac* database above. Contains four past years. Not included are *New York Times* and *Wall Street Journal*. Cumulated annually.
Documentation: Online user help. Paper documentation also included.

Name: **Le Pac**
Program type: CD-ROM public access catalog
Vendor: Brodart Automation
Cost: Consult vendor. Price is quoted based upon options, number of units, titles, and catalog copies, etc.
Hardware requirements: IBM and compatibles
Description: This online CD-ROM patron access materials catalog has several access options. Browse access allows author, title, and subject access. Any search term will take the user to the nearest point in the alphabetic catalog. This list may be scrolled up or down and a title selected. Bibliographic information on the title is then displayed on the screen. Express access is more sophisticated, allowing for Boolean search, right and embedded wild card truncation. It also allows search by location or combined access points, keyword, author, title, and subject. A search interrupt feature will stop a search at any time. "See" and "see also" references are found in the catalog. A help file is always available and may be customized by library staff.

A special interlibrary loan feature of *Le Pac* allows a microcomputer to be used as an ILL director. Requests can be stored here. The director is basically a sophisticated electronic mail switching system. It collects ILL requests and then routes them to all participating libraries. The system will send calls late at night, if desired, in order to not interfere with business hours. It also maintains a complete record of transactions: calling, errors, and exceptions conditions. Statistical reports include requests by classification and by library. A variety of request forms are also available, including serials, audiovisual, and monograph.

A circulation interface can interact with many library circulation control systems to display item status and other information.

Documentation: Excellent notebook contains hardware and software overview, tutorial, and reference. Each section contains review questions and exercise activities. Excellent index.

Name: **Magazine Index Plus**

Program type: CD-ROM database

Vendor: Information Access Company

Cost: $4,200, first year with hardware; $3,500, first year without hardware; school year subscription is $1000 less; $950, annual renewal; $950, backfile first year.

Hardware requirements: IBM and compatibles, with CD-ROM

Description: Public access terminal provides easy access to some 400 magazines of general interest. Range covers past three years with bibliographic data and, in some cases, brief annotations. Public can generally find its way around without staff assistance. The program is popular for quickly finding citations about homework assignment topics. Many of the magazines are also available as full-text editions in a related CD-ROM product, *Magazine Collection*.

Documentation: Onscreen help files for public use. Paper documentation also provided.

Name: **The Public Domain Software On File Collection on CD-ROM**

Program type: Public domain software

Vendor: Facts On File

Cost: $195

Hardware requirements: Apple II series with CD-ROM

Description: This excellent collection of software contains over 200 public domain programs on a CD-ROM disk. The disk cannot be altered by patrons and substitutes for 22 floppy disks in the collection for the Apple. All programs have been tested and debugged. Appropriate for school or public libraries. Contains business, graphics, utilities, miscellany, education, music, and home management categories. Educational programs include spelling improvement, equations, and more.

Documentation: 31-page manual

Name: **Webster's Ninth New Collegiate Dictionary**
Program type: Electronic dictionary
Vendor: Highlighted Data
Cost: $199.95
Hardware requirements: Macintosh
Description: This new CD-ROM edition of *Webster's* standard print version contains all and more of the original. Virtually all of the text and illustrations are included. Unlike the print version, however, the CD-ROM edition can pronounce the words. In addition, contents can be enlarged for better viewing and provide connections between related words.

Review sources: *Reference Books Bulletin (Booklist)*, June 1, 1991, 1891.
Documentation: A short users manual explains how to install search software in the Macintosh system folder and how to get started.

Children's Services and Children's Library Skills

Microcomputer software will do more than administrative work. For years now, librarians have employed it for educational purposes, both for library skills and for general education. It is far beyond the scope of this book to offer selections for such areas as general education development (GED), resume preparation, or English as a second language. Some areas specifically related to library work, such as reading referral, reading club tracking, and readability calculations are included.

As for the library skill software, it has long been suggested that it is very boring. A lot of strides have been made in this area in the past five years. Some of the packages for creating word puzzles and crosswords are truly excellent, automating chores that librarians have done manually for decades.

The software described in this section will:

Generate specialized lists
Gauge reading levels of written materials
Assist in library instruction
Create word-find, crossword, and other puzzles
Test reading materials
Track reading club participation.

Name:	**Almanacs**
Program type:	Library skills
Vendor:	CALICO
Cost:	$29.95
Hardware requirements:	Apple II series
Description:	Suitable for grades 3–6. Introduces students to use of different types of almanacs. Thirty-six screens allow both forward movement and review of any page at any time. Multiple-choice and scramble puzzles are used throughout to make program interactive and enhance learning. Positive reinforcement boosts learners' morale. Projects for further study are listed at end of program.
Documentation:	Self-documenting

Name:	**Bartlett's Familiar Quotations**
Program type:	Library skills
Vendor:	CALICO
Cost:	$29.95
Hardware requirements:	Apple II series
Description:	This delightful program gives good instruction for *Bartlett's*. Material is presented in 36 screens of explanatory text and multiple-choice questions. Students may flip to any page from any page, making review quick and easy. The program uses no negative aspects to the learning situation, just positive reinforcement. Material is divided into a description of *Bartlett's*, hints on its use, information on how it is indexed, and a special section on the next edition. If the student answers enough questions, a free ride on ''Bartlett's Balloon'' is awarded.
Documentation:	Self-documenting.

Name:	**BookBrain**
Program type:	Reader referral
Vendor:	Oryx Press
Cost:	$195 per module (multiple copy discounts available)
Hardware requirements:	Apple II series
Description:	Reading referral database contains some 2000 titles used to direct kids to materials appropriate for their age and interest. Written by E. A. Hass (Dr. Rita Book), a children's radio program figure, the program is engaging, personalized, and quite sophisticated. Children may explore books by subject, title, keyword, author, or by getting help from the book detective.
Review sources:	*Apple Library Users Group Newsletter*, April 1989, 63.
Related programs:	*BookWhiz*
Documentation:	64-page manual of instructions describing how the librarian or teacher can use the program to best advantage.

Name:	**BookWhiz**
Program type:	Reading referral
Vendor:	Educational Testing Service
Cost:	$199 for each module; three modules are available for grades 3 through 6, grades 6 through 9, and 10–12
Hardware requirements:	Apple II series; IBM and compatibles
Description:	This excellent and extremely easy-to-use program is available on three levels: grades 3–6, 6–9, and 10–12. Each set contains a program disk and a variety of subject category disks. The program allows users two basic choices: con-

struct a story or select a book. New users will usually want to construct the story first, giving them a chance to analyze their own interests. By choosing from a succession of menus, they very quickly define their interests into one or more of the subject disks (interests are rated by the computer according to the number of times they are displayed in the story lines selected during the process). The user may then select one of these subject disks or another disk.

Not all sets contain the same data disks. The grades 10–12 set contains a special disk called "Teen Problems"; the grades 6–9 disk contains one called "Growing Up—What It's Really Like." Other categories for both sets include adventure, history, romance, and others. The set for grades 3–6 is actually entitled "BookWhiz, Jr.," and contains "Growing Up," "Funny," and other subject disks. In asking for a selection of recommended books, users first input several criteria (e.g., male or female main character). The resulting list can be printed out.

The database may be modified by the librarian to reflect the library's collection. A printed list of all books in the program's original database is included with each set to make this chore much easier.

Related programs:	*Bookbrain*, above.
Documentation:	Small booklet, conveniently stored within plastic diskette box. Contains field-test results, backup procedures, operating instructions. Tells how to modify the database.

Name:	**Byte into Books**
Program type:	Reader advisory
Vendor:	CALICO
Cost:	$99.95
Hardware requirements:	Apple II series
Description:	For grades 1–8, this program provides suggested reading lists based on students' quiz responses. Input are grade level, gender, interests, reading ability, and enthusiasm. Information about over 500 children's books is available from the program. An alphabetic list of matches, personalized with the child's name, contains author, title, shelf location and annotation. Statistics are also provided by the program, such as tallies on each category of book (e.g., mysteries) and the number of children and grade levels using the program. The program can be customized by the librarian.
Documentation:	Manual contains complete information and guidelines for use.

Name:	**Call Number Order (Dewey and Fiction)**
Program type:	Library skills
Vendor:	CALICO
Cost:	$24.95
Hardware requirements:	Apple II series
Description:	To be used as a tutorial to introduce new employees to the Dewey system, the program can also be used for students or general public. Will handle both review and testing.
Documentation:	The simple booklet is all that is needed.

Name:	**Crossword Magic**
Program type:	Puzzle Maker
Vendor:	Mindscape, Inc.
Cost:	$49.95 (includes backup disk)
Hardware requirements:	Apple II series; Commodore; IBM and compatibles
Description:	This program automates production of crossword puzzles, just as *Puzzles and Posters* (described below) automates the production of word-find puzzles. There are differences, however. *Crossword Magic*, while simple to operate, is not as straightforward as *Puzzles and Posters*. To create a word-find puzzle, it is necessary only to enter a word list, then wait a few moments for a puzzle to be printed. A crossword puzzle requires not only a word list but clues as well. *Crossword Magic* will not make perfect puzzles by itself (i.e., they will not look like newspaper puzzles), since the areas between words are filled in with random letters. Planning and editing in the program's manual mode, are therefore necessary to dress it up. The resulting puzzles, though they will not look exactly like those in a newspaper, are excellent.

Working with the program is fun, in the same way solving a crossword is fun—but backward. The program creates a specified size, or expands its grid to accommodate all words as they are entered. The program holds words that won't fit in a special buffer, where they remain until they do fit, when they pop out to expand the puzzle dramatically. Puzzles may be 3 to 20 boxes across and down. It is best to make a list of words on paper first, especially if a topical puzzle is being created. Feed in most important or longest words first, and fit the last words manually (if necessary). Puzzles may have 80 or more words, or as few as desired. Making a puzzle takes 30 minutes, at most. One demonstration puzzle is included. Sound may be turned off.

| Documentation: | Program comes with two booklets: an operating manual (23 pages of start-up information, instructions, methods for creating good puzzles, and tips), and a manual that demonstrates how to create a good puzzle, with illustrations. |

Name:	**Current Biography**
Program type:	Library skills
Vendor:	CALICO
Cost:	$29.95
Hardware requirements:	Apple II series
Description:	This simple and easy-to-use program provides training in the use of the reference tool *Current Biography*. No earthshaking graphics or other frills, but it does the job.
Documentation:	Single sheet with prerequisites, teaching strategies, objectives, and directions for use, intended for librarian or teacher assistance.

Name:	**Electronic Bookshelf**
Program type:	Reading management
Vendor:	The Electronic Bookshelf
Cost:	$150, program disk; $45, titles disk; lab pack available
Hardware requirements:	Apple II series
Description:	This program can help people of all ages become more involved with reading. It is geared to elementary schools, junior and senior high schools, public libraries, college preparatory reading programs, developmental reading programs, adult education classes, and summer reading programs. Developers Rosalie and Jerry Carter had the collaboration of a number of teachers and librarians, including Eric Anderson, a well-known pioneer of microcomputers in school libraries.

The Electronic Bookshelf has three important functions: testing, recordkeeping, and scorekeeping of groups of students. Students are assigned to a disk. Each disk can handle up to 210 students and record the quiz results of 170 titles for each student. Up to 934 unique titles can be read and recorded by the total group. A large number of titles with quizzes are already included, but it is possible to add any new titles and make up quizzes as necessary. After reading a book, students or patrons take the quiz in the computer. The program compiles the scores, which may then be viewed by the one in charge of the program. An added benefit is that students also learn to use the computer for a database function.

Some of the books included in series I are: *Anything for a Friend; A Summer to Die; Tiger Eyes; Black Stallion; The Lion, the Witch, and the Wardrobe*; and *Twenty-one Balloons*. Series II includes: *The Accident; Letter Perfect; Snowbound; Tarzan of the Apes; The Yearling; Dragonquest; The Swiss Family Robinson; Sea Wolf; Candy Man; Durango Street*; and *Prince Caspian*. Some of the titles in Series III are *The Adventures of Tom Sawyer; Alas Babylon; Cheaper by the Dozen; Death of a Salesman; Nineteen Eighty-four; A Separate Peace; A Raisin in the Sun; The Ox Bow Incident*; and *Flowers for Algernon*.

Review sources: *Booklist*, October 1, 1985, 283;
School Library Media Quarterly, Spring 1986, 159.

Documentation: Notebook, containing complete procedures for setup and getting started. Also contains advice on planning a contest or project, and public relations.

Name: **Elementary Library Media Skills**

Program type: Library skills

Vendor: Combase, Inc.

Cost: $125 per module; $350 complete set (30-day return privilege)

Hardware requirements: Apple II series

Description: The most comprehensive microcomputer-based library instruction set available, in four modules (12 disks): "Discovering Available Resources" covers media resources and media classifications. "Locating Resources" teaches users about the card catalog and locating materials in the library. "Organization of Resources" covers alphabetical order, numerical order, and biographical order, and "Research and Study Skills" teaches basic reference skills and research skills.

The highly interactive program makes good use of graphics, puzzles, and riddles, and it is entertaining. Students select a specific area for study or can take the entire course in library skills. Lessons are straightforward, requiring no special knowledge or understanding of computers, and programs are self-paced, allowing students to stop to reflect at any point or to go back to a previous page. "Mickey Micro," a whimsical screen character, provides positive reinforcement.

Each lesson begins with a quick overview of material to be learned. The "Fiction" module, for example, allows students to pick separate lessons ("What Is Fiction?" "Call Numbers for Fiction," and "Call Number Game [for Fiction]").

Documentation: Reproducible worksheets in massive notebook, as well as list of educational objectives and suggestions for further learning and activities

Name: **Fiction Finder**
Program type: Reader advisory
Vendor: CALICO
Cost: $39.95
Hardware requirements: Apple II series
Description: Easy way to create booklists for individual library collection and to provide for differing interest levels. Provides customized lists of reading materials for patrons or teachers—up to 1000 book titles in 27 categories (such as westerns and romances). Each category may be classified eight ways (e.g., college level, long, short, easy reading). Materials selected by program may be printed out or viewed on screen.
Documentation: A small booklet, which explains all

Name: **How Can I Find It If I Don't Know What I'm Looking For: Reference Search**
Program type: Library skills
Vendor: Sunburst Communications
Cost: $65; lab pack of ten, $195
Hardware requirements: Apple II series
Description: For grades 4–9. Designed by Ann Lathrop, well-known pioneer of microcomputer use in libraries. This very-easy-to-use program will serve the elementary school librarian well in augmenting library skill instruction training. Program consists of three modules. The first is a simple four-screen description of the program. The second module teaches students how to find specific information in sixteen reference subject categories, such as sports, religions, and art. After choosing a topic the student is then asked for more detailed information, until a list of books can be given.

The final module gives individualized instruction on using various specific reference books. Ten types of books are listed, including encyclopedias, almanacs, atlases, etc. The student chooses a type and then sees a description of that type of book, plus a list of actual titles.

The editor mode allows the program to be altered to reflect actual titles available in library.

Review sources: *Booklist, Curriculum Product News*

Documentation: Notebook containing complete instructions. Contains reproducible worksheets such as crossword puzzles, reference search questions, etc., and data screens. Field test results are also given.

Name: **Library Catalog**

Program type: Library skills tutorial

Vendor: CALICO

Cost: $29.95

Hardware requirements: Apple II series

Description: Provides tutorial-style learning experience with the library catalog. Material is presented, and then student is questioned to see if the concepts have been learned. If not, the student must repeat the material. The user has complete control of the screens, and can go back or forward at any time.

Documentation: Short manual for startup, otherwise self-documenting

Name: **Library of Congress Call Number Order**

Program type: Library skills

Vendor: CALICO

Cost: $29.95

Hardware requirements: Apple II series

Description: Same concept as *Library Catalog*, but this program concentrates on teaching, reviewing, and testing the Library of Congress Classification system. Good for employees, students, and general patrons. For grades 10 to adult.

Documentation: The simple booklet is all that is needed.

Name: **Library Search and Solve: History**

Program type: Library skills

Vendor: K–12 MicroMedia

Cost: $29.95

Hardware requirements: Apple II series

Description: This module of the library research program is aimed at grades 4–10. It builds research skills in the area of history. For more details, see description of *Library Search and Solve: The Library Research Program*, below.

Name:	**Library Search and Solve: The Library Research Program**
Program type:	Library skills
Vendor:	K–12 MicroMedia
Cost:	$29.95
Hardware requirements:	Apple II series
Description:	The first (original) of four programs available for teaching library research skills to grades 4–10 (the other three are described below). Material for this program was developed by Uriel Winslow, media specialist at the William O. Schaefer School in Tappan, New York. Learning takes the form of a game in which the computer asks questions. The main computer screen looks a bit like a "Concentration" game screen, with nine numbered squares. Students pick the question that is represented by a square. If their answer is correct, a portion of a picture is revealed. Answers to questions are found in reference materials in the library. These materials may be placed near the computer for student use, or students may move through the library to find material (although there may be some confusion as to who is using the computer at a given time). The librarian may include other questions to customize the program to the library's own collection. As students answer the questions using library resources, they receive scores to rank them in the program's Hall of Fame. Upon completing all four units of this program (including the three listed here), a certificate of merit can be printed out. Uses high-resolution graphics and color screens. One drawback to the program is that it will keep track of only up to 75 students at one time.
Related programs:	See modules below.
Documentation:	Simple booklet describes getting started routines, provides hints for play, and contains a printout of certificate of merit. The booklet is not required for student use.

Name:	**Library Search and Solve: Literature**
Program type:	Library skills
Vendor:	K–12 MicroMedia
Cost:	$29.95
Hardware requirements:	Apple II series
Description:	This program tutors students in the use of library materials in literature. For more details, see description of *Library Search and Solve: The Library Research Program*, above.

Name: **Library Search and Solve: Science**
Program type: Library skills
Vendor: K–12 MicroMedia
Cost: $29.95
Hardware requirements: Apple II series
Description: This program tutors students in library skills in the area of science research. For more details, see description of *Library Search and Solve: The Library Research Program*, above.

Name: **Name That Book!**
Program type: Reading game (software and book package)
Vendor: Scarecrow Press
Cost: $42.50
Hardware requirements: Apple II series
Description: Book and disk package provides complementary features. Book contains over 1700 questions about children's books. It also contains rules for playing "Battle of the Books" game. Software has 600 additional questions that kids can answer for entertainment and information.
Documentation: Self-documenting

Name: **Periodical Indexes**
Program type: Library skills
Vendor: CALICO
Cost: $29.95
Hardware requirements: Apple II series
Description: Provides tutorial-style learning experience for *Periodical Indexes*. Material is presented, then student is questioned to see if they picked up the concepts correctly. If not, they must repeat. They have complete control of the screens, since they can go back at any time, or forward.
Documentation: Short manual for startup, otherwise self-documenting

Name: **Poetry Indexes**
Program type: Library skills
Vendor: CALICO
Cost: $29.95
Hardware requirements: Apple II series
Description: Provides a tutorial-style learning experience for *Poetry Indexes*. Material is presented, and then student is questioned to see if concepts have been learned. If not, the student must

repeat the material. The user has complete control of the screens and can go back or forward at any time.

Documentation: Short start-up booklet, otherwise self-documenting

Name: **Ripley's Library Skills**
Program type: Library skills multimedia set
Vendor: Society for Visual Education, Inc.
Cost: $219, software, filmstrips, tapes
Hardware requirements: Apple II series, filmstrip projector, cassette player
Description: For grades 4–6, and grades 7 and 8 remediation. The tapes ("Exploring the Library with Ripley's," "Starting Your Research on Ripley's," "Ripley's Introduces Other Sources," and "Confirming Your Ripley's Research") go with the four filmstrips. The two disks (four sides) are for beginners and advanced students ("Ripley's Beginning Library Research Skills" and beginning and advanced "Ripley's Using Other Library Sources"). Disk programs are a combination of quiz, game, and rewards. The object is to proceed through library, represented as game board, by answering questions about encyclopedias, almanacs, atlases, and other reference tools.

Everything is well done. Print is large and easy to read; catalog cards are displayed on screen for some exercises, allowing students to find call number, author, publisher, etc., for points. "Ripley fact" is displayed every question or two to help maintain interest and give reinforcement for correct answers. Some facts are animated (a wink or wave from Ripley character). Other graphics include set of encyclopedias and card catalog. Student must pick proper volume or drawer to answer a question correctly. System's disk management allows teacher to keep track of student's performance, as well as "save" student's place so he or she need not start at the beginning after a break.

Comes with complete set of catalog cards and labels. Comprehensive filmstrips include material about almanac, atlas, autobiography, bibliography, biography, call number, card catalog, classification system, dictionary, encyclopedia, fiction, index, nonfiction, periodicals, plagiarism, research topic, table of contents, title page, working list, and vertical file. Material and presentation are excellent, using color, interesting graphics, and logic to impart basic understanding of library skills. Each filmstrip has 50–57 frames, and the script for each filmstrip is given in accompanying guide. All materials are packaged in convenient binder.

Documentation: Manual with many reproducible worksheets for the four filmstrips

Name: **Skills Maker**
Program type: Library instruction authoring system
Vendor: Follett Software Company
Cost: $89.96
Hardware requirements: Apple II series
Description: One of new generation of library "do it" programs; students go to shelves to answer questions posed by computer. The program is an authoring system that allows teachers or librarians to produce printed exercises. It is not a hands-on program for students. Program can be customized to include only books that are actually owned by library). Books described include *Readers' Guide* (part 1 teaches author and subject entries; part 2, *see* and *see also*), almanacs, dictionaries, atlases, and encyclopedias.
Review sources: *Apple Library Users Group Newsletter*, December 1984, 22

Name: **Using an Index to Periodicals**
Program type: Library skills
Vendor: Combase, Inc.
Cost: $50 for each of two levels
Hardware requirements: Apple II series
Description: Microcomputer-based introduction to *Readers' Guide to Periodical Literature* on elementary and advanced levels. Both levels introduce information indexes, including an interactive tutorial on differences of the card catalog, magazine index, and back-of-book index. The elementary level has tutorials on the organization of *Readers' Guide*, its use, and special features, and a checkout test. For most part, the two levels cover the same ground, but the advanced level is aimed at the user who is already acquainted with the *Readers' Guide*. It has a checklist instead of a test. Good interaction and graphics throughout. Completion time is approximately 30 to 60 minutes.
Review sources: *Apple Library Users Group Newsletter*, April 1985, 32.
Documentation: Self-documenting. Reproducible worksheets for program include facsimile pages from *Readers' Guide*, self-tests, and research exercise accompanies each package.

Name:	**Where in Europe Is Carmen Sandiego?**
Program type:	Library research skill adventure game
Vendor:	Broderbund
Cost:	$44.95
Hardware requirements:	Apple II series; IBM and compatibles
Description:	Suitable for child or adult, this program is the third of four Carmen Sandiego role-playing games (see below for others). Players learn about Europe while trying to apprehend the notorious international jewel thief Carmen Sandiego and her gang. Play includes a lot of thinking in order to solve the mystery. The game is timed, and so players must work quickly. The program answers questions about the gang and other particulars from its database. Anyone will learn far more from this series than from playing arcade games!
Review sources:	*Run*, January 1989, 24.
	Commodore Magazine, August 1989, 18.
Related programs:	*Where in Time Is Carmen Sandiego?; Where in the World Is Carmen Sandiego?; Where in the USA Is Carmen Sandiego?*
Documentation:	Excellent brief manual of instructions of how to play the game

Name:	**Where in the USA Is Carmen Sandiego?**
Program type:	Library research skill adventure game
Vendor:	Broderbund
Cost:	$44.95
Hardware requirements:	Apple II series
Description:	For ages nine through adult, this is the second in the Carmen Sandiego series. Carmen, a notorious international jewel thief, must be found before her gang steals the Liberty Bell. Players take on the role of a detective with the program and use crime computer to solve the mystery. Along the way, they learn about other things. Included is a copy of *Fodor's USA Travel Guide*. Skills that are improved include U.S. geography—all 50 states plus the District of Columbia are traveled.
Review sources:	*MacWorld*, November 1989, 217.
Related programs:	*Where in the World Is Carmen Sandiego?; Where in Time Is Carmen Sandiego?; Where in Europe Is Carmen Sandiego?*
Documentation:	Excellent brief manual of instructions that explain how to play the game

Name:	**Where in the World Is Carmen Sandiego?**
Program type:	Library research skill adventure game
Vendor:	Broderbund
Cost:	$39.95
Hardware requirements:	Apple II series; IBM and compatibles; Macintosh
Description:	This was the first module in the Carmen Sandiego series of adventure games. The games have become exceedingly popular and are seen as a lively method of teaching library skills. Users play the part of a detective to apprehend the notorious smuggler Carmen Sandiego and her gang. Included is a copy of *The World Almanac*. Players learn fact-hunting skills and familiarity with a major reference source as well as world geography. Extremely well-done. For ages nine to adult.
Review sources:	*Computer Shopper*, September 1989, 572.
	Amiga World, October 1989, 16.
Related programs:	*Where in the USA Is Carmen Sandiego?; Where in Europe Is Carmen Sandiego?; Where in Time Is Carmen Sandiego?*
Documentation:	Excellent brief manual giving instructions

Name:	**Where in Time Is Carmen Sandiego?**
Program type:	Library research skill adventure game
Vendor:	Broderbund
Cost:	$44.95; $54.95 for school edition; lab packs available
Hardware requirements:	Apple II series; IBM and compatibles
Description:	This is the most recent in the Carmen Sandiego series of popular and educational role-playing games. Students learn about history and how to use library reference books. For ages nine to adult. Includes *New American Desk Encyclopedia* for tracking down clues. Players travel in twelve countries and use a time machine. Screen graphics are excellent, as are the clues and game. Stimulating and educational for any age group.
Review sources:	*Booklist*, May 15, 1990, 1822.
Related programs:	*Where in the USA Is Carmen Sandiego?; Where in Europe Is Carmen Sandiego?; Where in the World Is Carmen Sandiego?*
Documentation:	Excellent short booklet of instructions

Circulation Systems

The circulation systems described in this section, for the most part, stand alone. They are not full library systems for circulation and cataloging that include an online catalog. Even more important, many of them are geared to circulating only one type of media or material (e.g., textbooks). Libraries needing a more advanced or sophisticated system would be better served by the listings in the section on integrated library systems.

Two of the criteria for selecting a circulation system are the capacity and speed of the system. Ask the vendor about the base of installed users. How many libraries use their system? How long has it been around?

Name:	**Access.List**
Program type:	Circulation statistics
Vendor:	Real Time Computer Services
Cost:	$40 (plus $2 postage)
Hardware requirements:	Apple II series
Description:	Program will generate statistics for all or part of collection, special collections, periodicals, AV equipment, newspapers. The program is useful for the small library without access to a larger system that may already maintain such data. Materials to be analyzed are entered once. Each is assigned an access number by the computer. The user then records this number on the material. Each time an item is checked out, its number is entered into computer. Accumulated data is sent to screen or printer. A report will show access number, author, name, call number, and number of times circulated. The percentage of books in a range checked out once, twice, three times, etc., is also available. Access numbers can be written on paper first, then added as a batch to computer database later.
Documentation:	Five pages containing directions for computer setup and a complete description of various menu options

Name: **Auto Librarian Library Circulation Software**

Program type: Circulation system

Vendor: Highsmith

Cost: $199.95 (specify corporate or public library version)

Hardware requirements: IBM and compatibles, 20 megabyte minimum hard-disk drive

Description: The program is a simple system for keeping track of circulation, overdues, fines, and reserves. It can perform many tasks, but it will not read MARC records. It will also not network, so it can be used on only one terminal, making it useful only to smaller libraries, especially corporate and small public.

Holdings must be added and assigned an accession number. Each patron is assigned a borrower's code. Circulation periods are variable. Book and borrower codes may be quickly keyed in or entered with a bar wand (sold separately). Overdue notices may be created, using the system as a word processor. These notices may be batch printed with the overdue list (mailmerge) as first, second, or final notice. Fines owed are automatically calculated. Book search is by author, title, call number, book number or a simple subject. No Boolean search is supported. A report will tell if the book is missing, in, or out. Overdue alert is made when patron checks book out. The basic system, with its 20 megabyte hard drive, will hold up to 12,000 books and 2,000 patrons. The corporate version groups patrons by company departments. A portable barcode reader may be purchased separately for inventory. A list of missing books will then be available. The system includes a simple program called *Back-It* for backing up records.

Documentation: Manual of start-up instructions and suggestions

Name: **Circulation/Catalog Plus**

Program type: Circulation system

Vendor: Follett Software Company/Patron Access Catalog

Cost: $3,190

Hardware requirements: IBM and compatibles, with 3 megabytes of extended RAM, and 30 to 145 megabyte hard-disk drive

Description: Easy to use and install. Menu-driven system utilizes a barcode scanner. Will manage up to 65,000 items with full MARC records. Number of possible patrons depends upon the size and number of item records.

Special features include: inventory, status of items, circulation of temporary items, printing of more than 28 different lists, notices, and reports. A status window printout displays total items out, number of items currently overdue, number and amount of outstanding fines, number of items on reserve, number of patrons and items in system, highest barcode numbers used for both patrons and items, and day's total circulation. Can print, at any time, overdue notices, bills, reserve notices, and expired card notices. The system will also generate a complete list of patrons, titles, fines, reserves, and expired-card holders. Will provide circulation statistics by Dewey or LC numbers, special category, fiction by author, call number and number of circulations.

Data from Follett's catalog card program, *Quick Card*, can be uploaded to this system.

Review sources:	*The Computing Teacher*, November 1985, 49.
Related programs:	*Quick Card*
Documentation:	Excellent, brief manual of instructions

Name:	**Circulation Control**
Program type:	Circulation
Vendor:	Right On Programs
Cost:	$299
Hardware requirements:	IBM and compatibles
Description:	This circulation system for small libraries, created by a librarian, will work with hard-disk drive. Books can be entered into the system as they are circulated, which obviates a lengthy start-up time. A special, heart-shaped rubber stamp is included to mark each book as it is entered, so that there is no duplication. Information about patrons and materials are recalled by an identification number. The system will also generate overdue notices (available through Right On). Overdues are flagged as patrons try to check out books.
Documentation:	Notebook of procedures, instructions, and startup directions.

Name:	**Circulation Control Reserve**
Program type:	Circulation control add-on
Vendor:	Right On Programs
Cost:	$359
Hardware requirements:	IBM and compatibles, with hard-disk drive
Description:	Includes all features of *Circulation Control*, above, and adds the ability to reserve books for patrons. To reserve, patron's identification number and book identification number are entered into system.

Related programs: *Circulation Control*

Documentation: Notebook of procedures, instructions, and startup directions

Name: **Circulation Control Search**

Program type: Circulation control add-on

Vendor: Right On Programs

Cost: $399

Hardware requirements: IBM and compatibles, with hard-disk drive

Description: Includes all features of *Circulation Control*, above, plus the added feature of search in a variety of ways. Files can be searched by patron name or identification number, title, author, call number, or six subject headings.

Related programs: *Circulation Control*

Documentation: Notebook of procedures, instructions, and startup directions

Name: **Circulation Control Super**

Program type: Circulation system add-on

Vendor: Right On Programs

Cost: $439

Hardware requirements: IBM and compatibles, with hard-disk drive

Description: System provides all features of *Circulation Control,* above, plus a variety of others. Included in this package are circulation functions, reserve functions, and the ability to search the database in a variety of ways.

Documentation: Notebook of procedures, instructions, and startup directions

Name: **Circulation Plus**

Program type: Circulation system

Vendor: Follett

Cost: $895. Includes one year toll-free telephone support and upgrades. Additional support is available for $125 per year per site. Portable Scan Plus software included with package.

Hardware requirements: Apple II series, with 5 megabyte or larger hard-disk drive, ProDOS

Description: Uses barcode labels and scanner for checking library materials in and out. The menu-driven system comes in three versions: 15,000 items (4,000 patrons); 30,000 items (15,000 patrons); and 65,000 items (15,000 patrons).

       CircWorks Plus, an *AppleWorks* program, is included. This module tracks statistics bimonthly, semiannually, etc. It consolidates statistics for narrow interest ranges (such as Dewey 302s or books about autos) and tracks circulation range from month to month. Materials can be barcoded into the system as they are circulated to begin using the system immediately instead of the entire collection being entered at one time. Twenty-two patron types are supported and a sophisticated feature allows for five due dates. Data from Follett's catalog card program, *Quick Card*, may be uploaded to the system.

Review sources:	*Library Software Review*, July–August 1984, 247.
Related programs:	*Quick Card, Alliance Plus, Catalog Plus*
Documentation:	Excellent 150-page user's manual. Contains screenshots and examples of work.
Name:	**Circulation Plus** (MS-DOS version)
Program type:	Circulation system
Vendor:	Follett
Cost:	$895, standalone; $1,895, networkable. Includes one year toll-free support and upgrades. Additional support is available for $125 per year per site. Portable Scan Plus software included with package. Demonstration disk available.
Hardware requirements:	IBM and compatibles, 20 megabyte minimum hard-disk drive
Description:	Easy to use and install. Utilizes barcode labels and scanner, and is menu driven. Will accept up to 200,000 full MARC records. Maximum number of patrons depends on number of titles. Provides circulation and online public access catalog functions. Fully MARC compatible: data entry screens with 260 MARC tag for publisher, copyright date, and place of publication will store both ISBN and LCCN. Will print in both shelflist and call number order.

Twenty-two patron types may be entered, to assist in generating patron information. For example, at the end of a school year seniors can be purged with a single command.

System will provide information about inventory, item status, and circulation of temporary items. It will print over 28 different lists, notices, and reports, and provide a window display of total items out, number of items currently overdue, outstanding fines, number of items on reserve, number of patrons and items in system, highest barcode numbers for patrons and items, and the day's total circulation. It can also print overdue, reserve, and expired card notices at any time. Statistics can be provided by Dewey or LC division, special category, fiction by author, call number, and number of circulations. Supports creation of bibliographies with full or abbreviated entries using the catalog mode.

Review sources: *Library Software Review*, July–August 1984, 247.

Related programs: *Alliance Plus, Catalog Plus*

Documentation: Excellent 150-page user's manual contains screenshots and examples of work

Name: **Compucirc**

Program type: Circulation system for special libraries

Vendor: Embar Information Consultants, Inc.

Cost: Contact vendor for current pricing

Hardware requirements: IBM and compatibles

Description: This system was created for special libraries. Setup and installation is quick and simple. All fields come preselected for immediate use; custom needs may be addressed by altering these as required. System will integrate with *Compulog II*, an online catalog module. Major components include checkin and checkout of materials, placing of reserves, maintenance of overdues and recalls, notice production, and reports (including statistical reports). Collection usage may be tracked not only by materials but by corporate department as well. System is menu driven: reports and notices menu and utilities are displayed on the main menu; item information options, patron information options, and transactions and holdings options are displayed on a database maintenance menu. This is a fine circulation system for small libraries to consider. For any library with more than a few thousand volumes, however, a larger system should be considered.

Name: **Due List**

Program type: Overdue management

Vendor: Meadowbrook Middle School Library

Cost: $5 (public domain)

Hardware requirements: Apple II series

Description: This simple program performs a simple task—the tracking and management of up to 1,300 overdue items. They may be listed by due date, author, class, or student. Overdue notices can then be generated. The program is extremely limited, however, in that data cannot be corrected once it has been entered. Very easy to use.

Documentation: One page, which is all that is required

Name:	**Film Booking and Loan Control**
Program type:	AV circulation
Vendor:	Right On Programs
Cost:	$149
Hardware requirements:	IBM and compatibles
Description:	Film data is entered into system. When a film is requested, the request date is checked against those already in the system. Since the system does not allow for the same film to be booked twice at the same time, user is warned of conflict. The name of each borrower, title of film, cost, length of loan, due date, etc., are listed as the time to send materials nears. This list may be sent to screen or printer.

All films are given special identification numbers, the number by which the film will always be recalled when requested. Patron identification numbers are also given. Special reports include a list of film requests for specific locations and dates. A catalog of all holdings can also be printed out. Installation on a hard drive is quick and easy, completely automated at the touch of a key.

Documentation:	The simple, easy set of instructions is all that is needed. Much of the program is completely self-documenting.

Name:	**Library Circulation Manager**
Program type:	Circulation system
Vendor:	K–12 MicroMedia
Cost:	$199
Hardware requirements:	Apple II series
Description:	This circulation system for very small libraries and school libraries will handle up to 2200 patrons. A hard-disk drive may be used, or up to 200 patrons may be included on the program disk, for a total of 2200 patrons on five data disks plus the system disk. System will handle up to six checkouts per student, including returned items with outstanding fines. Fields include: home room (3 characters), names (17 characters), address (17 characters), items (32 characters each). Reports available include overdue notices by homeroom or student number, overdue report by homeroom or student number, fines outstanding by homeroom or student number, number of items outstanding, all items and fines by homeroom or student number, and the ability to search for an item. Utilities will generate overdue letters (text generated by user) and overdue slips. The letter-writing utility is

primitive; users might be better off generating letters and written materials with their usual word processor.

Documentation:	Notebook containing sample printouts, hints from other librarians, data entry, transactions, correcting, deleting students, reports, and utilities

Name:	**Library Circulation System III**
Program type:	Circulation system
Vendor:	Winnebago
Cost:	$995
Hardware requirements:	Apple II series
Description:	This popular system will assist small libraries with holdings of up to 60,000 items. System is simple and easy to use. It prints overdue lists and notices, calculates fines, and prints out inventory and missing materials lists. It will help inventory and has up to five material headings, four patron headings, and 32 material types. Can be used either manually or with a bar wand. System is MicroLIF-compatible.
Related programs:	*Library Circulation System II,* which will run on floppy-disk drives, serves up to 3500 patrons. Other related programs include *Computer CAT* and *Catalog Card Maker IV.*
Documentation:	Excellent manual of instructions and help

Name:	**Media Circulation System Program**
Program type:	AV circulation system
Vendor:	MecklerSoft
Cost:	$84.95
Hardware requirements:	IBM and compatibles; Macintosh
Description:	An easy-to-use program for creating a media circulation system. Program will record and modify AV holdings and their scheduling. Users may also create media confirmation, shipping, and overdue reports. Holdings can be searched by author and title as well as by transaction number, patron's name or organization, and inventory lists produced.
Documentation:	Notebook of examples and startup instructions

Name:	**Media Management System**
Program type:	AV circulation system
Vendor:	Video Inc.
Cost:	$3,250; hourly booking system, $1,500 additional
Hardware requirements:	IBM and compatibles, with hard-disk drive, 150-character–width printer.

Description: System provides a preformatted catalog and circulation system for AV materials. Fields for data entry include order number, title, location, media type, general subjects, specific subjects, level, length, production date, series title, author, annotation, language used, producer, distributor, fiction or nonfiction, publisher order number, video rights, expiry date, date purchased, etc. The system is especially good for libraries with large videotape or film collections. Booking system tracks materials for one calendar year. Statistical reports include history files on all media, as well as a history of overdue records by individual or location. Materials lists can be produced by general or specific subject, series, order number, alphabetical, and language type, and can be based on book materials, non-narrative materials, distributor, annotation, expiry date, media type. Reports will include an audit trail, daily reports to each shopping location or user, and daily operational reports (daily delivery list, packing sheets, location and user, shipping labels, daily overdue and due back list, update and return media materials).

Name: **Nonesuch Circulation System**
Program type: Circulation system
Vendor: Ringgold Management Systems, Inc.
Cost: $2,500 per terminal; demonstration disk, $90
Hardware requirements: IBM and compatibles, hard-disk drive
Description: Patron cards and material to be circulated are labelled with bar codes. Features include check-out, check-in, status inquiry, overdue notices printouts, reports of all types, and reserve materials. More than one terminal is supported.
Related programs: *Nonesuch Acquisitions System*
Documentation: Manual of instructions, startup, reference

Name: **Overdue Book Control**
Program type: Overdues
Vendor: Right On Programs
Cost: $99. Additional overdue paper forms are $52 for 1000.
Hardware requirements: IBM and compatibles; Apple II series (for school version only)
Description: Librarians can track overdue materials with a minimum of difficulty with this program. Three different versions of this program are available, based on how overdues may be identified. The "identification" version uses a personal identification number, and a numerical list may be generated. The

"name" version produces an alphabetical listing. In the "school" version, fields such as student, teacher, homeroom are available. The program is simple to use. Data is entered as required and a printout on multi-copy, continuous feed overdue notices (included) is generated. Options include: create a new entry, change or delete an entry, print overdue notices, print entire list, change data disk, and make new data disk.

Documentation: Easy-to-understand booklet of information

Name: **Overdue Collector**
Program type: Overdues
Vendor: Follett Software
Cost: $42.95
Hardware requirements: Apple II series
Description: A companion program for *Overdue Writer, Overdue Collector* automatically collects active records from *Overdue Writer*. They can be cumulated on one disk. As compiled, program will print additional notices, bills, master lists, or room lists. Can also be cleared as materials are returned.
Related programs: *Overdue Writer*
Documentation: Booklet of instructions

Name: **Overdue Writer**
Program type: Overdues
Vendor: Follett Software
Cost: $129.95
Hardware requirements: Apple II series
Description: Simple system for writing overdue notices. A predefined, ready-to-go database. Information about unreturned items is entered into database. Program then prints lists of patrons as well as first, second, and third notices and bills. Recommended for a library with less than 500 checkouts per average week.
Related programs: *Overdue Collector*
Documentation: Excellent manual of instructions

Name: **Textbook Plus**
Program type: Circulation
Vendor: Follett Software
Cost: $1,295
Hardware requirements: IBM and compatibles, 10 to 20 megabyte hard-disk drive

Description: This excellent circulation system for textbooks is aimed at school libraries that must keep track of large numbers of textbooks loaned to students. This barcode-based system uses a scanner. System can be accessed through network options and from multiple terminals. It will either stand alone or it can be integrated into *Circulation Plus*. Its 20 fields include textbook title, author, ISBN, number of copies on hand, number checked out, edition, copyright, publisher, school department that purchased book, note, additional materials with text, vendor's name and address, vendor's phone, budget category, basic or supplementary text, price, state adoption year, district adoption year, circulation period and courses. Each transaction record contains textbook bibliographic record number, student name, copy number, teacher's name, period, checkout date and due date.

Related programs: *Circulation Plus*

Documentation: Booklet of simple instructions

Name: **Winnebago Circ**

Program type: Circulation

Vendor: Winnebago Library Software Company

Cost: $995

Hardware requirements: IBM and compatibles, with hard-disk drive and 2 megabytes for each 1000 entries

Description: System permits circulation of up to 200,000 entries to 50,000 patrons. Includes special textbook control feature for schools. Hundreds of material types can be entered. Stores MARC records. Records can be searched by subject, title, or patron name. System will print overdue lists and notices on cards or paper, list of materials checked out to date, reserve lists and notices, statistical reports. Fine tracking system handles unpaid overdues until paid. Multiple network stations permitted.

Related programs: *Winnebago CAT, Union Catalog*

Documentation: Manual of instructions

Communications and Online Database Systems

Communications programs can provide a variety of services as well as short cuts to many otherwise tedious jobs.

Calling a database service means entering a telephone number with a modem, gearing your computer to the parameters of the service, remembering a password, and often much more. A telecommunications package such as *Smartcom*, once programmed, will do all of those things with the touch of a key. With a telecommunications package, a computer may store whole search strategies and routines. Some will even provide online help for accessing various databases, such as *Prosearch*.

A few communications programs can be used directly by the public, such as *Search Helper*. With this package patrons can call up a database, obtain search results, and print material without the librarian being involved.

Another service, the electronic bulletin board system (BBS), offers a way for libraries to network with each other as well as to offer a dialup service to their patrons. A BBS can provide off-hour information services, feedback, and a way to post communications.

Name:	**Biblio-Link for Pro-Cite**
Program type:	Direct record transfer from online databases (BRS, Dialog, MEDLARS, MUMS, NOTIS, OCLC, RLIN, SCORPIO)
Vendor:	Personal Bibliographic Software, Inc.
Cost:	$195 per module; separate module for each database
Hardware requirements:	IBM and compatibles; Macintosh
Description:	Reformats downloaded records directly for use with *Pro-Cite*. Separate programs are available for BRS, Dialog, LS/2000, OCLC, NOTIS, MUMS, SCORPIO, MEDLARS. After an online search, records that have stored in a file may then be processed by *Biblio-Link*. *Pro-Cite* may then be employed to sort, search, edit, and index all processed records. Records from different database (i.e., records with different formats) may as a result be easily processed and edited in the

same database with no manual conversion necessary. Program is quite versatile and flexible. BRS module will work with BRS, BRS After Dark, and BRS/BRKTHRU and will recognize 141 database names and 186 field names. Additional field and database names can be entered as required. Dialog module will recognize 650 database numbers and 28 fields. MEDLARS module will recognize 29 databases and 279 data element mnemonics or fields. OCLC module works with 350 MARC fields and subfields.

Related programs: *Pro-Cite*

Documentation: Separate manuals for each utility. Contains illustrated instructions for customization, error messages, and a tutorial.

Name: **Cleaner and Makecd**

Program type: Download utility

Vendor: MecklerSoft

Cost: $59.95

Hardware requirements: IBM and compatibles

Description: Simple program for downloading and cleanup of online search results. Will work with most online services. Once results have been downloaded, they can be cleaned up with this package.

Documentation: Easy-to-use manual of instructions

Name: **Crosstalk XVI**

Program type: Communications

Vendor: DCA/Crosstalk Communications

Cost: $195

Hardware requirements: IBM and compatibles

Description: Potent and popular communications package offers a wide variety of features, including excellent file transfer and a script (programming language) for advanced users wishing to make the most of the program. The program is easy to learn and use, because its command structure has few esoteric characters or words.

Review sources: *InfoWorld*, May 8, 1989, 52.
PC World, June 1989, 149.

Related programs: *Crosstalk for Windows*

Documentation: Manual of instructions

Name: **ERIC MicroSearch**

Program type: Online search tutorial

Vendor: Information Resources Publications

Cost: $50, set (includes program disk, one database disk, and user manual); $7.50, individual disks: program disk, educational technology, computer literacy, microcomputer hardware and software evaluation and selection, resources for library instruction, basic skills, and library and information science. Additional disks sent as part of subscription service or sold separately ($10 each).

Hardware requirements: Apple II series; IBM and compatibles

Description: This program is the local answer to the high cost of teaching telecommunications. Program makes available a limited number of ERIC records that can be searched just as if the user were actually online. Although not as useful as the real ERIC, the program does provide good instruction, especially to younger users. It is also perhaps a first and very inexpensive way for anyone to start their online experience before going on to the real thing. Boolean operators, printing, etc., can all be done with this program.

Review sources: *The Computing Teacher*, March 1985, 62.
School Library Media Activities Monthly, June 1989, 39.

Documentation: Self-documenting

Name: **HyperACCESS**

Program type: Telecommunications

Vendor: Hilgrave, Inc.

Cost: $149

Hardware requirements: IBM and compatibles

Description: Of particular note about this program is its ability to emulate various terminals: Wang VS2110, IBM3278, VT-52, VT-100, VT-220, VT-IBM3101, TV950, TTY, H19, and ANSI terminals. Its proprietary protocol can compress and decompress files in real time, giving the user the potential to send files at up to five times the modem baud rate. The program has password security. It is an excellent program for most general purpose online management.

Review sources: *InfoWorld*, December 7, 1987, 53.

Documentation: Manual of instructions, which includes search worksheets

Name: **The Major BBS**

Program type: Bulletin board system

Vendor: Galacticomm, Inc.

Cost: $59, two-line system; 4, 8, 16, 32, and 64 at $359, $659, $959, $1,259, and $1,559. Other packages available upon request.

Hardware requirements:	IBM and compatibles
Description:	While this package can be purchased and configured for only one modem line, it is designed for multiline use up to 64 modems. It is a well-conceived and designed system, containing a wide variety of features and capabilities.
Sources of information:	*Catalog of Add-on Software for the Major BBS.* Available through Galacticomm, Inc. Booklet highlights more than 75 products from 10 companies that can be used to enhance the basic Galacticomm system, including games, billing, database use by more than one person, etc.
Related programs:	See manufacturer's catalog of add-on software
Documentation:	Excellent book, describing operation of system, setup, and more

Name:	**Pro-Search**
Program type:	Terminal package
Vendor:	Personal Bibliographic Software, Inc.
Cost:	$495; sample disk available for $19.95 with user manual and 3 online hours; quarterly update, $150 per year
Hardware requirements:	IBM and compatibles; Macintosh
Description:	This spectacular front-end package will not only provide a host of significant features for online searchers of Dialog and BRS, but it will save most users online time charges as well. The package, once programmed with user identification and passwords, will allow the user to automatically log on with just a few keystrokes. The program will make an automated search, keep an accounting record of time and charges, and create invoices for patrons. Search strategies may be formulated and saved offline and then used online. Help is always available online, too. Menus can be altered to help the novice or expert searcher.

Special feature areas can be purchased separately to make the BBS function as a shopping mall or an entertainment area (graphics and arcade) and to change menu choices for different levels of users, such as to make the system more user friendly for a beginner.

Users select the database they wish to access. Each database is represented on an electronic card that contains an abstract of online charges, nature of database, etc. Because abstracts and database go out of date quickly, disk updates may be purchased quarterly or annually. Data disks cover biology and medicine, art, education and social sciences, business, government and news, and engineering, mathematics, and physical sciences. Utilities disk is separate. Data saved with the buffer may be coded for later use with a word processor or other application.

Review sources: *"Pro-Search* Simplifies DIALOG and BRS Searching," *American Libraries*, December 1985, 825.

Related programs: *Biblio-Links*

Documentation: Notebook details system's capabilities and explains configuration routine and advanced utilities.

Name: **Procomm Plus**

Program type: Communications

Vendor: Datastorm Technologies

Cost: $50

Hardware requirements: IBM and compatibles

Description: A substantial feature of this system is its dialing directory. It supports up to 200 computers that can be accessed by just pressing a key. Thirteen standard error-checking protocols for the exchange of data are also supported by the system. Baud rate support ranges from a lowly 300 to a potent 115,200 (which requires a modem that will operate at that rate). A special "host" mode permits unattended operation of the system, allowing users with other computers to call your system up in the middle of the night and transfer files, send electronic mail, or do other work. The system contains a programming language for advanced users. *Procomm Plus* will emulate 16 terminals.

Review sources: *Personal Computing*, April 1988, 173.

Documentation: Manual of instructions

Name: **RBBS**

Program type: Bulletin board system

Vendor: Capital PC-SIG User Group

Cost: $8

Hardware requirements: IBM-PC (compatibles not acceptable)

Description: This user-supported, low-cost electronic bulletin board system has been used successfully in libraries to some extent for public use, but with great success for interlibrary loan.

Documentation: Excellent manual is included

Name: **Red Ryder Host BBS**

Program type: Telecommunications

Vendor: FreeSoft Company

Cost: $80

Hardware requirements: Macintosh

Description: Popular communications program for the Macintosh performs a variety of functions. With the mouse, a user can easily communicate with other computers via modem. Files can be saved or downloaded using many error-checking protocols, including XModem, MacBinary, YModem, Kermit, and CompuServe's B. Screens may be scrolled to memory and then pulled back as needed. The number of such screens can be set according to the user's requirements. Handles macros as well. The system is quite versatile and will accommodate the novice as well as the most advanced users with friendliness.

Review sources: *Macuser*, December 1987, 152.
MacWeek, November 3, 1987, 54.

Documentation: Instruction manual of basic procedures

Name: **Simulate.exe. the Online Simulator**

Program type: Online training aid

Vendor: MecklerSoft

Cost: $59.95

Hardware requirements: IBM and compatibles

Description: This program offers the capability of simulating online searches. Can be used as a training aid for classroom demonstrations and study or as practice by a user before actually going online when time is at more of a premium. Will transform a downloaded online search into BASIC. No programming experience required.

Documentation: Manual of easy-to-follow instructions

Name: **Smartcom II**

Program type: Terminal package

Vendor: Hayes Microcomputer Products, Inc.

Cost: $149

Hardware requirements: IBM and compatibles; Macintosh

Description: *Smartcom* is an impressive package that will originate and answer calls; create, list, receive, or send a file; manage parameter; turn a printer on and off; and do much more. The program is totally menu-driven and easy to operate and will print a screen at any time. *Smartcom* will store and dial several dozen phone numbers, with a full complement of parameters for each, making one-finger operation a reality.

The Macintosh version provides the same excellent utilities with the convenience of the mouse. Icons across the bottom of the screen let the user choose printer control, editing, dialing, disk functions, etc.

Review sources: *Online*, November 1990, 36.
Link-up, September–October 1990, 24.

Related programs: An advanced version, *Smartcom III*, is available for $249, with additional features for IBM and compatibles.

Documentation: Excellent tab-indexed manual, with complete installation and operation instructions

Name: **Wildcat BBS**

Program type: Bulletin board system

Vendor: Mustang Software, Inc.

Cost: $129, one connection; $249, up to ten connections; $499, up to 250 connections.

Hardware requirements: IBM and compatibles

Description: An excellent system, especially for the security conscious. This multiline system will handle up to 250 callers simultaneously if it is connected to a LANtastic local area network. Supporting ten different data exchange protocols, the program is fairly simple to operate, and many custom options permitted.

Review sources: *Link-up*, March–April 1991, 18.

Documentation: Excellent manual of customization options, startup procedures, and other practical advice

Database Management

There is a wide variety of database management software from which to choose. The software falls into two basic categories of database managers (sometimes called file handlers) and database management systems. The managers, while powerful, generally restrict users to one file at a time; management systems permit several files to be in use at one time. The systems are also harder to learn, and they may even contain their own special programming or command language to permit the user to program them into a very sophisticated package, such as a circulation system. Such programming has been done by librarians, though it has been stated again and again in the literature that librarians should be apprehensive about doing in-house programming. It should not be attempted unless someone is well versed in the particular program being used.

Database programs can be used to create files of all sorts, including ready-reference, community facts, and local history indexes. They are widely used to maintain and track small collections of special materials.

A database may consist of one or more files. Each file contains a group of records. Each record is made up of fields. For instance, a database of materials may contain two separate files: books and AV. The books file may contain the fields: title, author, subject, and ISBN. The books file may be sorted or searched by any of these fields. Sorting and searching, as well as the use of Boolean operators, capacity, and other characteristics differ among systems, so once again it is a good idea to take your time before purchasing a database system.

The essential aspects of the creation and maintenance of a database are collecting data, designing the database, entering the data, editing the database, and revising and updating the data as needed. Obviously, it is necessary to purchase a software package at some point before the database is created.

Major differences among programs include the ability and speed in sorting files, record capacity, field length and number, indexing, flexibility in data entry, and formatting to make reports to paper and screen.

Some of the uses for which a database system is being used in libraries include:

Information and referral (automated card file)
Inventory

Book orders
Career catalogs
Mailing lists
Newspaper indexing
Personnel lists
Periodical lists
Phone lists
Phone survey
Friends of Library files
Summer-reading club participants
Local organizations
Community file lists
Union lists of large-print books
Videotape catalogs
Wall chart for public reference.

Name:	**AskSam**
Program type:	Database manager
Vendor:	Seaside Software
Cost:	$200
Hardware requirements:	IBM and compatibles
Description:	Excellent system for entering and managing randomly entered data. *AskSam* will sort even single characters or whole paragraphs as required. Built-in word processor allows for creation of files, which can be dumped into the database component and then sorted. Easy and popular program used by librarians.
Review sources:	*Personal Computing*, April 1989, 200. *InfoWorld*, April 17, 1989, 78.
Documentation:	Easy-to-follow book for handling most questions

Name:	**Bookends**
Program type:	Reference card file
Vendor:	Sensible Software, Inc.
Cost:	$99
Hardware requirements:	Macintosh
Description:	This program uses HyperCard, a special Macintosh system for organizing data. HyperCard programs are called stacks, and *Bookends* is, hence, called stackware. The size of each database is limited by the amount of disk space. Its major use will be the storing and printing of bibliographies. Ready-made fields include author, title, editor, journal, volume, pages, date, publisher, location, keywords, abstract,

and classification. Each category may be as long as 30,000 characters. Files may be merged or imported from any tab-delimited text file. The program can also be used to retrieve data from the online utility Dialog. Alphabetical listing of authors and keywords can be generated. Macintosh version creates a journal glossary to make it easy to enter journal names in multiple places. Boolean searches are possible as well as searches by whole words, characters, and strings by a single or multiple categories. Can send output to a word-processing program or to a text file. Works with *Multi-Finder*. Not copy protected. An excellent program for use with a ready reference desk.

Related programs:	*HyperCard, MultiFinder*.
Documentation:	Detailed notebook contains examples of major functions. Indexed.

Name:	**dBase IV**
Program type:	Relational database management system
Vendor:	Ashton-Tate
Cost:	$795; $995, local area network edition; $30, upgrade from *dBase III*
Hardware requirements:	IBM and compatibles
Description:	*dBase*, one of the very first relational database systems for microcomputers, has long been a popular product. Ashton-Tate has maintained its excellence through the years with several major updates, making it still a major leader. *dBase*, like many major database systems, can be used as a file management system. Users can employ the sophisticated command language that comes with it. Librarians have used *dBase* to program for many types of work, including circulation systems, serials, and much more. Manufacturers have used it to create software packages, which are then sold separately. The difficulty with the library staff creating software packages from scratch is the amount of skill and time that is required. The system can be used to create data entry forms.

On one level, *dBase* is easy to use. Anyone can install the system, create a database structure, and begin to input data in just a few minutes. The list that is created may be indexed, and reports can be generated. The report format is trickier, but eventually it becomes clear. However, the *dBase* program is not user friendly. Its popularity lies not in its excellent list-handling capability and enormous power, but in its programming language. By creating command files, which look and act like computer programs (e.g., BASIC or Pascal), a user can produce a program of immense power and sophistication. However, this programming structure causes many problems. Libraries that use *dBase* report that it is necessary to have someone on the staff who is proficient in programming.

dBase can be used without special knowledge, however, as a system for creating and manipulating data files directly. Name and address files, videotape files, even files of books and other media, can all be created without too much trouble. Sorting and relating databases can take more time, but the rewards of using *dBase* are sufficient to make it worthwhile.

dBase is so widely used that many *dBase* programs are available from many sources. Ashton-Tate, publishes a catalog of such programs called *Application Junction*. Meckler Publishing Corporation has also issued an entire volume on *dBase* programs specifically designed for libraries, *Essential Guide to dBase III in Libraries*, and another on *dBase IV*.

Review sources:	*Byte*, May 1990, 117
Related programs:	*Essential Guide to dBase III+ in Libraries "On Disk"*, described below
Documentation:	*dBase*'s eight manuals include full reference

Name:	**Disk Publisher**
Program type:	Electronic publishing system for CD-ROM or floppy disk distribution
Vendor:	KAware
Cost:	Contact vendor for current pricing
Hardware requirements:	IBM and compatibles, hard-disk drive (mass storage device must be at least three times greater than the size of the anticipated file).
Description:	System is designed for a small operation that needs to create its own CD-ROM product. There are four separate packages available, on full-text information, fielded information, image files, and graphic files. Each may be purchased separately, but all come with a copy of *KAware2 Retrieval System*.

With this system, it is possible to create your own database using in-house or external sources of data entry, and then prepare the disk for distribution. In the case of CD-

ROM, a manufacturer would produce the disk from information contained in the locally produced database.

Review sources: *Information Today*, November 1989.

Documentation: Notebook containing principles of disk publishing procedures. Separate sections on modules and *KAware2 Retrieval System*.

Name: **Essential Guide to dBase III+ in Libraries "On Disk"**
Program type: *dBase* programs
Vendor: MecklerSoft
Cost: $44.95
Hardware requirements: IBM and compatibles
Description: This program is for use with the database management system, *dBase*. Many important library functions can be improved with its use, making it unnecessary to create many programs from scratch. Package includes both book and disk. The book contains explanations and printout of programs, and the disk contains ready-to-run programs. Contents of the program include mailing list management, bibliographies, community resources file, newspaper indexing, abstracts, serials union list, reference archive, acquisitions, serials control, library catalog, catalog card production, registration, overdues, reserves, circulation, statistics, and bulk loans.
Related programs: *dBase*
Documentation: Volume contains discussion and printout of each program

Name: **InMagic**
Program type: Database
Vendor: InMagic
Cost: Contact vendor for latest pricing
Hardware requirements: IBM and compatibles
Description: *InMagic* (main program) allows text records of variable length, fields may be any length, and reports may be custom formatted. Though designed for special libraries, the database can perform many functions in public, academic, or school libraries. *InMagic* allows Boolean operators for searching, keyword or term indexing on any field, unlimited number of records in database, online help screens and tutorials, and flexible report generator for custom presentations. An annual user service contract can be purchased for 10 percent of the package price, and includes program updates.

Biblio, a separate library-specific package, will produce

an online catalog, an orders database with serial control and circulation data. *Orders*, an acquisitions module of a full-service system, provides full tracking of acquisitions, beginning with purchase request. It monitors receipt of order, tracks budget expenditure, sends status requests and claims to vendors, and creates status reports. Activity and backup reports may be generated. At appropriate time, cataloging information may be sent to main database, called *Catlog*. The system prints bibliographies, book and spine labels, shelflist cards, and inventory control printouts.

Serial module, besides producing routing slips, holdings lists, and title and subject bibliographies, maintains a file of subscription costs and names to which they are charged (and much more). *Circ*, a circulation control and management module, tracks items lent to persons from a corporation library. *Catlog*, an online catalog management system, provides an unlimited number of subject headings, location codes, classification numbers, contract numbers, and spine label information.

Related programs:	*SearchMagic* (patron access catalog); *MARC Adaptor* and *Multi Adaptor* (conversion tools).
Documentation:	*InMagic* comes with excellent manual of several hundred pages, well organized, clearly written, and indexed; includes glossary, data structure documentation worksheet, and installation procedures.
Name:	**IZE**
Program type:	Database management
Vendor:	Persoft Inc.
Cost:	$445
Hardware requirements:	IBM and compatibles, with hard-disk drive
Description:	*IZE* is a new type of product, organizing information that is largely randomly generated, such as text files from a word processor, or that has been downloaded from an online service. *IZE* can produce keyword indexes and find material quickly and easily. If you already have large data files that you would like to organize and use more fully, this is the database to consider. Online help screens provided are context sensitive.
Review sources:	*Library Software Review*, May–June 1989, 165. *InfoWorld*, October 30, 1989, 62.
Documentation:	Several manuals include the basic instruction manual, the printer manual, and the tutorial

Name:	**Member Tender: Membership Management System**
Program type:	Specialized database system
Vendor:	MecklerSoft
Cost:	$95
Hardware requirements:	IBM and compatibles, with 10 megabyte or larger hard-disk drive
Description:	This excellent program for tracking library friends and similar membership organizations will handle approximately 1000 records per half megabyte of available disk space. A database of more than 5000 members would be better served by a more sophisticated system, such as *dBase* or *Foxbase*. In *Member Tender*, a database may contain name, address (two lines), city and state, zip code, year, organization category or code, and interest group code. Tracking contributions and donations is very simple. A mailing list can be generated by the program, but a special privacy function can inhibit this feature. Twelve formats are provided for reports. Only the phone report can generate a report with phone numbers. Alphabetical reports and category reports are also possible. Menu windows make selection of choices convenient. The program must be installed on a hard-disk drive from distribution disks. Once copied, all files required for operation can then be accessed from the hard-disk drive.
Documentation:	Notebook contains detailed instruction for setup, utilities, choices, reports, and statistics. An appendix lists possible error messages and their meanings, with examples.

Name:	**Nutshell Plus**
Program type:	Relational database manager
Vendor:	IRIS Software Products
Cost:	$295
Hardware requirements:	IBM and compatibles
Description:	*Nutshell Plus* is much liked by its followers because of its ease of use. Setting up two databases and linking them together with the zoom feature is very simple, as is installation of the program.
Review sources:	*Library Software Review*, March–April, 1991, 142. *Computer Shopper*, December 1989, 248.
Documentation:	Excellent manual begins with introductory concepts in database management

Name:	**PC-File**
Program type:	Database manager

Vendor:	Buttonware
Cost:	$59.95
Hardware requirements:	IBM and compatibles
Description:	This easy-to-use and highly popular database manager has certain limitations, but is nevertheless an exceptional buy for the price. Affordable by all libraries, this shareware package will handle only one file per database, and up to 32,767 records per file. Each field may have 65 characters.
Related programs:	*PC-Write, PC-Talk.*

Name:	**PC-File/R**
Program type:	Relational database management system
Vendor:	Buttonware
Cost:	$149
Hardware requirements:	IBM and compatibles
Description:	Extension of *PC-File*, above. Will handle up to 42 files per database, 32,767 records per file, and can handle 1665 characters per field. Fields per record is 42.

Name:	**Pilot.exe**
Program type:	File management
Vendor:	MecklerSoft
Cost:	$59.95
Hardware requirements:	IBM and compatibles
Description:	This program will facilitate display and navigation of text files. Program chains together text files that the user has created. Information can be linked in various ways. Program's suggested use is for training manuals, or reference assistance.
Documentation:	Notebook of instructions

Name:	**Pro-Cite**
Program type:	Bibliography production
Vendor:	Personal Bibliographic Software, Inc.
Cost:	$395
Hardware requirements:	IBM and compatibles; Macintosh
Description:	In addition to bibliography production, *Pro-Cite* allows for two user-designed workforms, full-text searching, unlimited keyword searches, full Boolean logic (including NOT), sorting by any field (including "intelligent" data sorting), faster operation, and greater editing capabilities. Searching may be made by any field or by specific field, with or without truncation, and by word, number, standardized date,

workform type, or record number. Program uses ANSI as default for bibliographic style, simulates American Psychological Association or American Science Association style, or users may construct their own style. Files may be saved to disk in standard ASCII format for further preparation with standard word processor. System may be used to import and reformat data from Dialog, BRS, OCLC, and RLIN with corresponding *Biblio-Link* package. Other features are on-line help file, variable length fields and records, detection of duplicate records (including immediate deletion option).

Review sources: *Library Software Review*, March–April, 1989, 91.
Library Hi Tech News, February 1988, 355.
Related programs: *Biblio-Link*
Documentation: Illustrated notebook describes the system and uses.

Name: **R:Base System V**
Program type: Relational database management system
Vendor: Microrim, Inc.
Cost: $700
Hardware requirements: IBM and compatibles. Program is not generally compatible with RAM-resident programs, such as *SideKick Plus*.
Description: This database management system, similar to *dBase* in scope, is gaining widespread popularity among certain segments of the library profession. It can be used for online catalogs, online search records, acquisitions, accounting, etc. It can be manipulated from the prompt (similar to the *dBase* dot), as well as to write a program. Programs can be created from the Applications Express module, without being programmed. There is also a menu mode of operation that makes the program acceptable for beginners.

A Gateway Module allows for data import to and export of *1-2-3* and *dBase*. It will also work on a local area network with up to three simultaneous users.

Review sources: *Library Software Review*, January–February 1989, 24.
Documentation: Hands-on tutorial included in excellent manual. Command dictionary is separate manual. Instructions for conversion to and from other programs are also included.

Name: **Status IQ**
Program type: Text retrieval system
Vendor: CP International, Inc.
Cost: $2,000
Hardware requirements: IBM and compatibles

Description: *Status IQ* is an excellent text retrieval information system, allowing for very powerful search techniques, flexibility, and a wide range of uses. The database that is maintained by the user can be modified by adding articles and editing existing material regardless of original format (disk, online, word processor, etc.). It can be used to create an online catalog. All data contained in the database can be searched using Boolean logic. Once information is found, it can be reviewed or changed from any available workstation. "Hits" are weighted according to usefulness.

Desktop Publishing and Graphics

A lot has occurred in the area of computer graphics in just the past few years. It has, in fact, become a big industry all by itself. Desktop publishing refers to the ability to create camera-ready documents with a computer, materials that can go directly to a commercial printer without the need for a typesetter. The best desktop publishing requires a laser printer, but impressive results can be obtained even without one.

"Desktop publishing" systems can perform a multitude of functions, including borders, newsletters, and much more. Systems for creating and designing just about any type of graphic, including newsletters, stationery, banners, books, pamphlets, pictures, and just about anything else include *PageMaker* and *Ready, Set, Go!*

There are also simple, single-task packages that may create something impressive, but are limited. Individual tasks can also be accomplished by using programs such as *Bannermania, Print Shop*, and *Crossword Magic*. These programs will create banners, crossword puzzles, and other things, but they cannot design newsletters or make other, more sophisticated representations. They are good, but they are not suitable for all occasions or all libraries.

Purchasing a desktop publishing package is just the beginning. A multitude of clip art packages are available to add more variety and sophistication to the system. Special clip art programs with library themes are also listed below.

Name:	**Bannermania**
Program type:	Banner maker
Vendor:	Broderbund
Cost:	$34.95, IBM and Apple II; $69.95, Macintosh; lab packs available
Hardware requirements:	Apple II series; IBM and compatibles; Macintosh
Description:	Outstanding and extremely easy-to-use program produces exciting banners in a variety of styles, shapes, and fonts at the press of a button. Once a message has been entered, the

program will display a selection of banners one after the other until a choice is made, and then prints out the result.

Review sources: *PC Today*, July 1990, 60.
Closing the Gap, October–November 1990, 38.

Documentation: The 40-page instruction manual is all that you will need.

Name: **Border Clip Art for Libraries**

Program type: Graphics accessory

Vendor: LEI, Inc.

Cost: $52.75

Hardware requirements: Macintosh, with hard-disk drive

Description: Useful program of accessory graphics items specifically geared to libraries. Includes 80 borders and 42 clip art images. All images are stored in encapsulated Postscript format. The graphics require some eight megabytes of storage space on a hard-disk drive. Once installed, they may then be sized according to need.

Review sources: *Apple Library User Group Newsletter*, July 1990, 77

Documentation: The 21-page manual includes small reproductions of the artwork and borders.

Name: **Certificate Maker**

Program type: Graphics

Vendor: Springboard

Cost: $39.95

Hardware requirements: Apple II series; IBM and compatibles; Macintosh

Description: While a certificate could be made using many other graphics or desktop publishing programs, this one is specifically geared to do the job quickly and efficiently. Many borders and details are ready to go and can be punched up with only a few keystrokes. Over 200 template designs are provided. After selecting a certificate style the user adds a border and enters the name of the recipient and achievement. The user can also choose from 36 seals and stickers to append to the certificate. If identical certificates are going to several people, program allows user to insert different names into same certificate. With the "name wildcard" feature, a name can be inserted anywhere in the text of the message. The user creates a name file with several names, and the program then substitutes one each time it prints out the certificate.

Documentation: Excellent manual provides not only step-by-step instructions, but a complete illustrated directory of program certificates, borders, and other options.

Name:	**Easy Pages** (for *PageMaker*)
Program type:	Template package for use only with *PageMaker* (purchased separately)
Vendor:	MecklerSoft
Cost:	$59.95
Hardware requirements:	Macintosh
Description:	This easy-to-use template set provides ready-made page designs that can be used for creating library newsletters and other publications. If it is installed with public access computers, patrons can also use it. Program provides mastheads, regular column space, and much more. Finished article or text is added, and the program sizes and spaces the material accordingly. Five separate designs are included for newsletter production and for books.
Related programs:	*PageMaker*
Documentation:	Notebook of instructions and suggestions

Name:	**Easy Pages** (for *Ready, Set, Go!*)
Program type:	Template package for use only with *Ready, Set, Go!* (purchased separately)
Vendor:	MecklerSoft
Cost:	$59.95
Hardware requirements:	Macintosh
Description:	Easy-to-use template for the desktop publishing program *Ready, Set, Go!* Can be used by library staff or patrons to create newsletters, journals, or books. Once form is chosen, text from article is simply added to the template and automatically sized and spaced by the program, ready for printing. Spaces for regular columns, mastheads are provided. Five designs for newsletters, four for books included.
Related programs:	*Ready, Set, Go!*, above.

Name:	**Library Magic**
Program type:	Graphics printing
Vendor:	McCarthy-MacCormack, Inc.
Cost:	$49.95
Hardware requirements:	Apple II series
Description:	This low-cost and extremely simple-to-use program provides a variety of useful graphics capabilities. Functions include bookmarks, award certificates, library forms, and bookworms. Two choices are available for library forms. Users may generate readymade overdue notices with date, name, teacher or room, date due, and title and comment

spaces. These notices can be designed with a variety of graphics (e.g., an angry face, ALA national symbol, or many other icons). Special forms for many other uses may also be created, such as book reserve notices, library cards, receipts, etc. Several dozen cute bookmarks will help to brighten up the library area. Award certificates will be useful for the summer reading or other programs and can be awarded to library helpers, storytellers, library skills champions, and more.

Documentation: Short booklet with illustrations of many possible products. Instructions given as well, though few will be needed.

Name: **The New Print Shop**
Program type: Desktop publishing
Vendor: Broderbund
Cost: $59.95, IBM; $49.95, Apple
Hardware requirements: IBM and compatibles; Apple II series
Description: This program is one of the most popular that has ever been produced. It has sold well over one million copies, the first microcomputer package with that distinction. It has also been steadily and constantly improved by the manufacturer. *The New Print Shop* provides a variety of excellent and easy-to-use functions, including banners, calendars, posters, and greeting cards. A variety of fonts are available, plus over 100 images of high-resolution, good-quality artwork. The new system allows changing fonts and moving around within the program more easily. Posters can be created in cells and then pasted together to form giant posters. Double-width banners can be created.

There are lots of things that this program cannot do, however. It does not produce camera-ready page layouts. But the many things it does do cannot be outdone by other programs. It also now features a full onscreen preview option.

Review sources: *PC Publishing*, April 1990, 57.
Classroom Computer Learning, April 1990, 10.

Documentation: Excellent manual with illustrations of artwork, suggestions, and startup instructions

Name: **PageMaker**
Program type: Desktop publisher
Vendor: Aldus Corporation
Cost: $795

Hardware requirements: Macintosh; IBM and compatibles, with 20 megabyte hard-disk drive; Apple LaserWriter or other Postscript printer

Description: This is the most popular full desktop graphics package available for the IBM. Excellent for newsletter or magazine page layout, it will provide variable column width on same page. Other features include built-in library of borders and fill patterns. These templates can be used to create a wide variety of camera-ready artwork. Text files can be created with any word processor and then transferred to *PageMaker*.

Review sources: *PC World,* October 1988, 156.
PC Magazine, December 27, 1988, 126.

Related programs: *Easy Pages*

Documentation: Impressive set of manuals for installation, suggested uses, and much more

Name: **Publish It! 3**

Program type: Desktop publisher

Vendor: TimeWorks

Cost: $99.95, Apple; $199.95, IBM; $395, Macintosh

Hardware requirements: IBM and compatibles; Macintosh; Apple II series

Description: This highly sophisticated desktop publishing system creates camera-ready copy. The program in many ways falls midway between the power of *PageMaker* and *The New Print Shop*. It is able to produce first-rate results for most users' needs. Features include word processing, page layout, and many excellent graphics. System allows resizing all layout items (text, graphics, etc.) with ease. Also included is a large dictionary and thesaurus for word processing needs. Contains automatic installation program.

Review sources: *Home-Office Computing*, November 1990, 88.
Library Software Review, July–August 1990, 248.

Documentation: Thorough manual of detailed instructions for installation, learning how to navigate the system, and finding commands

Name: **Puzzles and Posters**

Program type: Puzzle Maker

Vendor: MECC

Cost: $59, Apple; $49, IBM

Hardware requirements: Apple II series; IBM and compatibles

Description: Products from this program are suitable for use with any age group. Word puzzles on any theme and in various sizes can be created in a few minutes. Disk contains four programs: Word Search, Crossword Puzzle, A-maze-ment, and Posters and Banners. Although many new programs do these things, this program still does the basic job very well. Word puzzles are created in three simple steps: (1) the user chooses a set of up to 50 words; (2) the words are entered with the keyboard, as prompted by the computer or permanently stored on data disk; and (3) the computer creates the puzzle. The puzzle may be printed out on either a stencil or spirit master. The program also generates the answer sheet. Smallest puzzle is 3×3 characters; the largest is 23×25.

The crossword puzzle component does not have nearly the power or flexibility of *Crossword Magic* (also reviewed in this volume), but it produces a crossword puzzle. An Imagewriter printer produces the best looking crossword puzzle. Results from other printers are not as elegant and should be used only as a pattern for creating final puzzle.

Posters and banners may be printed with this program, but it has neither the clip art, flexibility, nor quality of *The New Print Shop*.

Documentation:	The 36-page looseleaf binder has complete instructions, illustrations, and examples and screenshots of completed work.
Name:	**Ready, Set, Go!**
Program type:	Desktop publisher
Vendor:	Letraset
Cost:	$495
Hardware requirements:	Macintosh
Description:	This is one of the most outstanding desktop packages available. It is widely used and supported. Plenty of clip art can be used with it. Installation and learning take a very short period. Useful for anyone with moderate to advanced graphics needs.

System provides for complete camera-ready page layouts. It includes word-processing capability and import of files from other programs. This program may be just slightly less sophisticated than *PageMaker*, but it is sufficient for almost any size library with almost any desktop needs. It is also easier to use than *PageMaker*. Beginners can grasp most of the fundamentals and begin creating page layouts without too much trouble.

The system also has word processor spelling program, automatic wordwrap, and a glossary function.

Review sources:	*Library Hi Tech News*, April 1988, 16.
	MacGuide Magazine, Fall-Winter 1988, 244.
Related programs:	*Easy Pages*.
Documentation:	Instruction manual contains installation instructions, and system for creating camera-ready copy

Name:	**Springboard Publisher**
Program type:	Desktop publisher
Vendor:	Springboard
Cost:	$139.95, Apple; $129.95, IBM; $199.95, Macintosh
Hardware requirements:	Apple II series; IBM and compatibles; Macintosh
Description:	Extremely easy-to-use desktop publishing program. *101 Software Packages* included Springboard's *Newsroom*. Since then, desktop publishing has moved ahead by great leaps. Springboard has also moved ahead with this newly introduced product, which is excellent and uncomplicated for the person with limited time and budget. The features include page layout, word processing, and graphics. Very little setup is required in order to design a page, since the program will allow for many default characteristics. Up to nine columns may be generated per page, all different sizes if required.
Review sources:	*Personal Computing*, September 1989, 194.
Documentation:	Good manual, though you will rarely need it

Government Documents

Tracking government documents has always been a problem. A program to help check in such documents has been developed by libraries and is listed in this section.

Name:	**GOVDOX**
Program type:	Government documents check-in system
Vendor:	MecklerSoft
Cost:	$69.95
Hardware requirements:	IBM and compatibles
Description:	Easy system for any library needing to keep track of government documents. It is a compiled *dBase III* program (dBase not required). The database records documents with SuDoc, item number, title, date, subject term, and note. Retrieval is by SuDoc number, title, or subject.
Documentation:	Notebook with complete instructions

HyperCard

HyperCard, a new type of database system offered by Apple Computer for use with the Macintosh computer, promises connectivity. Connectivity promises a free flow of information within context by a HyperCard-based computer program.

Name:	**HyperCard**
Program type:	Database
Vendor:	Claris
Cost:	Included in price of a Macintosh computer
Hardware requirements:	Macintosh
Description:	*HyperCard* is an applications package that allows for the creation of hyperstacks, or stackware. Stacks can be created by the user or obtained, through vendors and public domain just as other programs have always been obtained.

Its basic function, as with most software, is to store information and relate it in several ways. The aspect that makes *HyperCard* unique is its ability to store and recall text, charts, and pictures in multiple ways. A *HyperCard* database is easily related to a stack of cards which can be advanced forward, backward, and sideways (randomly). This is why it is referred to as "stackware,"—each database is seen as a stack of cards. These cards can have any type of information on them, even digitized photographs.

A classic example of a library use of *HyperCard* is one created by several libraries, including the library of the Apple Computer Company. They created a stack of cards for an automated tour of the library. Patrons could "see" the library in the computer, ask questions, point to areas of interest, and explore as they desired—all without involving the librarian.

Documentation:	Excellent detailed manual with illustrated examples, commands, and methods for creating your own stackware. Many additional manuals are available from different publishers as well.

Name:	**Hyperties**
Program type:	Hypertext authoring system
Vendor:	Cognetics Corporation
Cost:	$349
Hardware requirements:	IBM and compatibles
Description:	Librarians may be interested in creating their own hyperstacks or stackware, instead of purchasing them or obtaining them from other *HyperCard* users. Using this program, it is possible to obviate some of the work involved in programming a new stack.
	Authoring systems are not new. They merely automate some of the often complicated procedures and write program code more quickly. This system uses an author component to generate and link documents. The browser component is used by the reader of the database. This system is very easy to learn and use, requiring little in the way of documentation. Most of it can be figured out during use of the program.
Review sources:	"Hypertext Authoring System," *Library Software Review*, January–February 1991, 74.
Related programs:	*HyperCard*
Documentation:	An excellent manual provides overview of system, tutorial, and system for planning a database.

Indexing

Many libraries have indexing projects, the most common being a local newspaper index for the local history collection. Occasionally, a library will index certain magazines to help users trace articles on topics for research papers.

Name:	**Authex Plus**
Program type:	Periodical indexing system
Vendor:	Reference Press
Cost:	$125; demonstration disk, $30; templates disk, $30
Hardware requirements:	IBM and compatibles
Description:	*Authex Plus* is an updated and improved version of the original *Authex*, which appeared in 1984. The new system has a large number of features and is suitable for many library tasks involving indexing. This menu-driven system's major function is to index periodicals, and according to the documentation can be "used effectively to prepare vertical file indexes, current awareness reports, newspaper indexes, special collections catalogues, and bibliographies." *Authex* employs an online authority file that accommodates subjects, names, and associated cross-references. Each heading is stored only once in the database. System also provides multiple-level subheadings and adds unlimited cross-references automatically. Some obvious uses include indexing topical magazines and newspapers for local history collections.

Authex Plus provides for up to four levels of subheadings, geographic subheadings, user-defined output formats, full screen editor, onscreen thesaurus, multicolumn output option, international characters, global find and replace, data import and export, online database searching, context sensitive help screens, and automatic blind reference checking.

The system allows for an unlimited number of subjects

only limit on file size. Database entries are allowed 16 fields maximum and 8192 characters per record, and field length is also limited. The authority and main databases may have variable-length records.

Documentation: A 126-page book of examples, illustrations, and techniques for getting the most out of the program

Name: **Magazine Article Filer**
Program type: Indexer
Vendor: Right On Programs
Cost: $99
Hardware requirements: IBM and compatibles
Description: A good program for reference librarians who need to maintain a ready reference file of articles. Each entry in the database includes space for its date, article title, author, publisher, ten subject fields, two user fields, and two comment files. Once material has been entered (only those fields required need be filled in) the program allows corrections. Any entry may be edited or deleted. A search by identification number, date, title, author, subject or user field may be made to the screen or to the printer. A versatile program under easy-to-use menu control.
Documentation: Simple booklet

Name: **Publication Indexer**
Program type: Index program
Vendor: Right On Programs
Cost: $85
Hardware requirements: IBM and compatibles
Description: This program is offered as a method for maintaining an index both for periodicals that do not provide one and as a stop-gap measure until the index of other periodicals arrives at the library. It is particularly suited to special libraries requiring access to current periodicals and for local newspaper indexing. The program is easy to use and menu-driven. Articles are entered at the prompt with title, magazine name, date, page numbers, two subject headings, and an annotation.
Documentation: Simple booklet

Integrated Library Systems

Integrated library systems represent an effort to bring together a number of library tasks into a single system, allowing the library more direct control over all of its automation with greater efficiency. For instance, while it is possible to purchase and use a catalog card production system, a bibliography generator, and a circulation system as separate packages, they may not share data and may even require different computers. An integrated library system on the other hand may allow the user to create a catalog card set, circulation records, and an online catalog all from the same data entry.

Name:	**The Assistant**
Program type:	Integrated library system
Vendor:	Library Automation Products, Inc.
Cost:	$2,300 per module for single user; $2,800 per module for multiple users; $350 to $400 annual maintenance per module; $1,000, MARC exchange utility; $1,000 multiple location exchange. A demonstration disk for cataloging and circulation and one for serials control, acquisitions, and fund accounting are available at $75 each, or $100 for both, with a portion applicable toward full purchase price.
Hardware requirements:	IBM and compatibles, 10 megabyte hard-disk drive minimum
Description:	Designed for small to medium-sized libraries, *The Assistant* provides a full range of services: cataloging, circulation, serials control, routing management, subscription renewal and budget projections, and acquisitions accounting. (Four megabytes of hard-drive disk space per 1000 bibliographic records.)
Documentation:	Massive binder containing detailed step-by-step instructions with screenshots for each module

Name:	**Automated Library System**
Program type:	Integrated library system

Vendor: The Foundation for Library Research, Inc.

Cost: $1,195

Hardware requirements: IBM and compatibles

Description: System offers a host of features for the small to medium-sized library, including the ability to link branch libraries. Other features include color screen, generation of 35 different lists, overdue reports, audiovisual material handling, bibliography creation, customizing the help screens, preparing reading histories, making catalog cards, inventory, and much more. It also has built-in security, passwords, and backup program options.

Name: **Card Datalog**

Program type: Integrated library system

Vendor: Data Trek, Inc.

Cost: $2,450 for each of four modules: cataloging, circulation, acquisitions, serials

Hardware requirements: Apple II series; IBM and compatibles

Description: This *dBase III* program provides a library system for cataloging, circulation, acquisitions, and serials. Easy-to-use system will create catalog cards, an online catalog with Boolean searching, spine and book labels, and reports by author, title, and subject. Acquisitions module will track orders from initial selection to final payment, including the creation of order letters and reports. It will also automate periodical orders. Serials function will print route slips, maintain list of no shows, and print renewal alerts. Circulation features include overdues, reserves, inventory, reports, and much more. System circulation information can be keyed in, or a bar wand can be used. The system cannot interface with CD-ROM, provide for ILL functions, or print bibliographies.

Name: **Columbia Library System**

Program type: Integrated circulation system

Vendor: Columbia Computing Services

Cost: $1,095, circulation module; contact vendor for prices of additional modules

Hardware requirements: IBM and compatibles

Description: Provides a complete library system for circulation, online public access catalog, acquisitions support, serial maintenance, and a MARC interface when combined with the acquisitions, catalog/OPAC, serials, MARC interface, and other modules. Will store up to 150,000 records.

Name: **Galaxy**
Program type: Integrated library system
Vendor: Gaylord
Cost: Contact vendor for current pricing
Hardware requirements: IBM and compatibles with CD-ROM drive
Description: *Galaxy* is a fully integrated system with modules to perform all major functions in a library. Based on MARC record format, the system contains *SuperCAT*, a CD-ROM system of 3.5 million LC MARC records for retrospective conversion and cataloging of materials. Another module is a very capable circulation system. It provides a full range of item control, and check-in and check-out procedures and options. It automatically calculates fines and includes holidays or other exceptions, and records show outstanding fines to limit patron privileges. Patron holds on titles may be placed. Circulation reports can be made by day, month or year. Special report generator will produce custom reports. Financial audit of circulation desk activity is also available. Lost or missing items report, purchase alert reports, overdue notices, billing notices, and hold or reserve notices also may be prepared. Circulation system also contains security code feature to limit access to sensitive data.

The cataloging module of the system uses MARC records and permits the use of LC MARC database for searching records for building database. Records may be edited and saved. Original records may also be created. Spine and pocket labels, catalog card sets, and shelflist cards can all be generated. Bibliographies can be generated from completed records for new book lists, etc.

The patron access catalog module is easy for patrons to use. Help is available through marked function keys and is context sensitive. Multilingual screens can be displayed. Screens may also be custom formatted. A guided search option will take patron through search routine step by step. Advanced search options use NISO command language. Boolean search may be made for author, title, subject, keyword, ISSN, and ISBN. Search can also be defined by format, publication date or language, partial or whole word. Search strategy help and hints appear on screen. Search results will immediately tell if item is on the shelf, checked out, due date, and other information.

Reserves, interlibrary loans, and holds may all be managed with the *Galaxy* library system.

Gaylord also offers retrospective conversion and database preparation services. Gaylord can upgrade non–MARC to full MARC II format.

Documentation:	Extremely detailed manuals offering suggestions for use, import of files, use with a LAN, and much more

Name:	**LibrA**
Program type:	Multilingual integrated library system
Vendor:	Ivy Systems Limited
Cost:	Contact vendor for current pricing; demonstration program, $20
Hardware requirements:	Macintosh
Description:	Provides all major library functions in a fully integrated system for small to medium-sized libraries. Multilingual capability makes it a strong option for libraries whose patrons speak more than one language. Five sections of program accommodate acquisitions, cataloging, circulation, referencing, and administration. It is multi-user, provides keyword extraction and search, supports standard card formats such as MARC and SMARC, and also provides telecommunications for electronic mail and for using online services such as Dialog. The manufacturer claims that the program is useful for both high-end and low-end market libraries. Password security system may be employed as needed. The acquisition subsystem creates selection cards for books, journals, and other media. Orders may be placed and tracked within the system to maintain current status and payment. The cataloging subsystem adheres to *AACR2*, if required. Circulation subsystem will send overdue notices, reserve books, calculate fines, and maintain patron records. The referencing subsystem (online catalog) provides for Boolean searching.
Documentation:	The user manual is illustrated with screenshots. It is well organized and contains individual sections on over 60 separate functions. Startup, acquisitions, cataloging, referencing, circulation, and administration of the system are major subdivisions of the manual.

Name:	**The Library System**
Program type:	Integrated library system

Vendor: Bar Scan, Inc.

Cost: Contact vendor for current pricing.

Hardware requirements: IBM and compatibles; will work with bar code scanner or keyboard

Description: Once the program is installed on a hard-disk drive, titles, patrons, and copy numbers must be entered and bar codes placed on cards and books. Circulation management may then begin. The bar codes on materials and patron cards are scanned. The return menu function checks materials back in. The system will indicate if any returned material is on hold so that it may be set aside. The fines mode will generate overdue notices or bills. Titles may be searched by author, call number, title, or subject. Up to eight subjects may be entered for each item. The system is also flexible enough to allow for a minimum fine and daily increment, a minimum fine plus a maximum daily increment, or a fine based on the cost of the item borrowed. Reports for statistical needs can be printed. These include the catalog, patrons, overdues, fines, and holds. The main advantages of this program are great simplicity and ease of use, both for setup and for daily use. There appears to be no way to expand the system beyond the basic circulation system.

Documentation: Notebook containing instructions, suggestions, and installation procedures

Name: **LION (Library Information ONline)**

Program type: Integrated library system

Vendor: CALICO

Cost: Based on collection size: $750, up to 10,000 titles; $1,050, up to 25,000 titles; $1,250, over 25,000 titles. Remote support package, $375 with modem, $150 for remote support software only. Separate and extra are Union Catalog module only, $450; Bibliofile Download Program only, $100; Barcode software and wand, $595. Other options and services available: inquire.

Hardware requirements: IBM and compatibles, with hard-disk drive. One megabyte of storage required for every 1,000 records anticipated in the database. Vendor suggests one patron search station for every 50 circulation items per day.

Description: This comprehensive system for creating online public access catalogs for patrons and circulation system is particularly suited for libraries with up to 250,000 circulation. System will manage a bibliographic database, create an index, and provide for user search of materials.

The LION circulation system is menu-driven and can be used with or without barcodes. Barcodes may be added later, if desired. Its basic menu provides for check-out, check-in, renew, hold, locate, print, discharge fines, change status, search catalog, quit. Circulation periods may be modified, but default system comes as 14 days (normal), 3 days (reserve), 30 days (extended), 7 days (brief), 1 hour (overnight), permanently out, special, and does not circulate. Ten different patron types are also supported and are named by library. A set of circulation rules (26 coded entries) comes with the system, but can be added to or changed as desired.

The database record, termed the bibliographic master record, will handle multimedia data records from 75 to 7,500 characters with 2 to 999 separate fields. Input of records can be made from a MARC-compatible disk, or menu or command driven manual entry may be used.

The search system is very easy to use. Patrons may search with single keyword for author, title, or subject. Boolean logic is also supported for multiple term search. The database may be searched by more than one patron workstation at a time if the system is networked.

In addition to the basic system, LION has several other options. Its inventory module allows a permanent record of holdings to be printed out. A barcode system may also be used to assist in circulation or data entry. The LION union catalog will allow multiple libraries to use the same database and to fully search holdings of all simultaneously. Patron workstations search only local library's collection, but the staff and circulation stations can search the entire union catalog.

MicroLIF option will convert MARC records to LION records. The vendor will also provide complete retrospective conversion service.

CALICO can provide hardware, software, and barcodes, and will load the database onto a hard-disk drive if both conversion and hardware are purchased.

Documentation: Comprehensive manual of instructions

Name: **Mac Library System**
Program type: Integrated library system
Vendor: Caspr

Cost: $1,695, single station; $4,995, multiple stations; $70, demonstration version, applicable towards full system purchase

Hardware requirements: Macintosh, with hard-disk drive

Description: Integrated system contains catalog, circulation, and acquisitions modules, and will make use of bar codes. Makes good use of the Macintosh menu and command structure. Provides easy access through pull-down menus and icons for catalog, budget, library vendors, patrons, circulation, and library serials. New data is easily added and may employ the Macintosh cut, copy, or paste features. The system will support up to 2 million records in each module.

The acquisitions module contains fund accounting and a vendor database for the entry of order information and the generation of purchase orders. It updates the catalog as items are received. Acquisition reports include status reports on all orders within a chronological period with full order details organized by charge code or patron; summary reports for orders within a chronological period that include the number of items ordered, supplier identification, and order totals; supplier analysis reports that list the number of orders for each supplier by date, total amount, outstanding orders, claims, cancellations, and 30, 60, 90, and 120 day order-response-time categories; outstanding order reports that list outstanding orders for a chronological period; order action reports that list orders invoiced by a supplier but not yet received; and a supplier report providing a complete alphabetical list of all suppliers.

The circulation module keeps track of patron records. It will check items in or out and put items on reserve. Patrons may be coded as P for general patron, E for employee, or S for Student. Library staff may assign library card numbers, or the system will do it automatically. It will print overdue notices, reserve placed notices, reserve available notices, and patron status notices. A report on reserve items by title, number of transactions by title, type, charge code, and call number, items on loan by document type, and items recorded as missing or lost can also be generated.

The catalog module will upload or import MARC and MicroLIF catalog records. It will also automatically create brief catalog records for items purchased. It is simple to use.The catalog can be searched by author, title, subject, or keyword. Terms may be combined with Boolean operators *and, or,* and *not.* Search terms may be truncated to a minimum of two characters. A search may also be limited by media type, such as AV. Bibliographies can be generated from such a search and used in a word processor for later editing. Other options are printed catalogs by author, subject, or shelflist order, and catalog cards.

Related programs:	*MacLap* (library patron access program), *MacCards*
Documentation:	The demonstration manual (all that was sent for review) is well-written, illustrated, and well-organized, and is undoubtedly some indication of the full manual. Separate sections treated the catalog, circulation, serials, and acquisitions modules.

Name:	**MacDewey**
Program type:	Online catalog and circulation system
Vendor:	Mousetrap Software
Cost:	$79.95
Hardware requirements:	Macintosh
Description:	Provides library catalog and circulation system. Can generate lists of overdue books or those borrowed by patrons. Flexible loan periods. Search for materials can be made by author, title, subject or fiction type. The program is quite a value for the dollar, but will be most useful to small collections and libraries.

Name:	**Micro-VTLS**
Program type:	Integrated library system
Vendor:	VTLS, Inc.
Cost:	Prices vary. Circulation module: $1,095, up to 500 patrons; $4,295, up to 100,000 patrons; cataloging module: $1,295, up to 2,000 items; $8,995, up to 160,000 items. Additional local area network charges. Discounts available for multiple sites of two or more. Annual support fee, $795. Annual license fees charged for single user or networked versions.
Hardware requirements:	IBM and compatibles, with 20 megabyte minimum hard-disk drive, barcode reader, tape backup system (optional)
Description:	Among its many features, this program will provide an online catalog, circulation, and statistic reports. The public access catalog may be searched by author, title, subject, series, utility control, number, local control numbers, ISBN, ISSN, LCCN, and call number. Right truncation of search terms is automatic. Search results are displayed in an easy-to-read menu. Circulation will handle renewals, patron searches, maintenance of fine and patron records, and it also

supports a sophisticated checkout period system. A data manager will let librarians modify and delete records containing bibliographic, authority, item, and patron data. System meets *AACR2* level 1 cataloging standards. Reports can generate circulation and bibliographic information, patron files, and controlled vocabulary terms. Multiple branch libraries can have all branches linked to a single database for complete up-to-date coverage for all. Training is available at the vendor's Blackburg, Virginia, headquarters.

Documentation: Massive binder of detailed explanations and instructions for operating the system. Each section gives excellent, step-by-step instructions for operations as simple as formatting a disk to backing up the system. Each section also ends with a user quiz to assist with training.

Name: **MOLLI**

Program type: Integrated library system

Vendor: Charles Clark Co., Inc.

Cost: $1,795, single user; $2,695, multiple users. Includes one year of support. Demonstration program free upon request.

Hardware requirements: IBM and compatibles, with hard-disk drive

Description: *MOLLI* is a fully MARC-compatible integrated library system providing the full range of library services. These services include circulation, online catalog, cataloging, keyword indexes, inventory, a wide range of reports, support functions, and security. The integrated online catalog and circulation functions provide search capabilities by any word or name. The status (circulating, on shelf, etc.) of any item can be easily obtained. Searching can also be multiterm and browsing. Full search allows up to three subjects, authors, notes, and titles to be combined. Boolean logic can also be employed. Bibliographies can be searched and printed out as desired.

Circulation functions include control of collections and maintenance of borrower's records, as well as usage statistics. Check-out may be made by keyboard or bar code reader. Reserves are signaled. Due date function is quite flexible, allowing for loan periods set by the librarian, or overridden by the librarian at the time of check-out. *MOLLI* will calculate all fines, or they can be overridden. The program will also generate overdue notices.

Inventory can be taken with a portable bar code reader for any part of the collection and makes use of the current circulation information already in the computer.

The system will generate reports on reserves list, accession list, keyword indexes, keyword lists, overdue status, cost of the collection, library usage, items on loan, lost-damaged items, missing items, and inventory conflict.

Review sources: *Library Software Review*, March–April 1987, 100.
The Book Report, September–October 1989, 8.

Name:	**PCemas Automated Library Management System**
Program type:	Integrated software for school library media center
Vendor:	ScholarChips Software, Inc.
Cost:	Contact vendor for current pricing.
Hardware requirements:	IBM and compatibles, 132-character printer. Compatible with local area networks: Novell Advanced Netware, 3Comm, and Token Ring.
Description:	Fully integrated modules contain acquisitions, local cataloging capability, circulation, inventory, budgeting, and an on-line student catalog. Library records can be maintained in MARC format. Catalog is searchable by subject, title, author, call number, title and key word, and with Boolean operators and *see* and *see also* references. The acquisitions system will track materials from request and order, payment vouchers, to receipt of materials. Library may establish different funds and maintain a constantly updated record of allocated, encumbered, committed, and available funds. The subject authority generator will supply up to 20,000 Sears subjects at no cost. It will also provide LC if necessary.
Related programs:	*PCemas Student Administration* package, containing scheduling, grades, and attendance records
Documentation:	System has detailed documentation that includes videotapes on how to install it and train patrons to use it.

Integrated Software

Integrated software must be loosely defined, since the term has been abused and misused by the media and manufacturers. It is sometimes casually slapped on any package label to help sell it. More than even a few years ago, more and more packages actually are providing more than one type of application. For instance, the word processing package *WordPerfect* will sort (a database function) and calculate (a math function). Desktop publishing programs will often do word processing. Many major packages routinely provide telecommunications programs. The line between types of software has grown very fine indeed.

Software in this section is considered integrated because it contains several major functions that work together in some way. This definition is particularly useful since the programs can be grouped here instead of being spread throughout this book. They are also not specifically library packages; they are "generic."

Functions differ from package to package, though the standard has been a word processor, spreadsheet, and database manager. Sometimes software contains a telecommunications package and graphics capability. How the functions work together also varies. For instance, some packages may share data, while others share a common menu for selection.

Some packages are far more powerful, not only in the individual capability of packages, but in the strength of their integration. A good example of this is in the integration of statistics and graphics. With some packages, the user creates a spreadsheet and the program will then use it to create a variety of graphic representations. The charts and graphs can then be automatically updated as material is changed or added.

One very exciting class of software is known as the desktop accessory. This type of program generally performs many functions that are associated with desktop work, such as notetaking, math, and scheduling. Some even perform integration features by allowing the flow of data from one program into another. Perhaps the most popular of these programs is *SideKick Plus*. Such programs are resident in the computer's memory and are summoned by the user from within (without exiting) other programs.

Another very special set of programs is called integrators, or do-it-yourself integrated software. These programs combine various software packages into a cohesive unit. The major advantage of integrators is that they can combine programs the library already owns so that it is not forced to switch to new, predetermined programs.

For example, one integrator, *DESQ*, works with virtually any IBM software, and can integrate up to a total of nine programs. Users may arrange their own menus and command structure. *DESQ* must have essential information, called agents, to run a program. A number of these agents come predefined, so that many programs can be up and running with little input from the user. *DESQ* also supports a mouse, if desired. It is also possible to transfer data between applications.

Systems such as *Windows* and the Macintosh graphic user interface also integrate software. It is easy to go from application to application and to exchange data.

There are some disadvantages to changing to integrated software. Probably most important is the need to relearn major programming skills, which might take a lot of time and cause some pain, especially if a software package has been in use for a long time. Another disadvantage is perhaps settling for less on some programs in order to get the integration. In some cases, it could even mean having to change or add computer hardware. If the library has functioned well using stand-alone packages, there may be no real reason to change.

Name:	**AppleWorks**
Program type:	Integrated software
Vendor:	Claris Corporation
Cost:	$249
Hardware requirements:	Apple II series
Description:	*AppleWorks* integrates database management, word processing, and a spreadsheet. It is possible to increase its capability by adding packages from other vendors, to include telecommunications, desktop publishing, and other enhancements.

AppleWorks is a very popular program because it is so easy to use. Within an hour of installation, most users can begin useful work, such as creating business documents. Many librarians have found this package extremely useful and just about all that they need for basic business chores. The package is fully menu-driven, with easy-to-follow menus for each function.

A file must be created for each function, which means data cannot be transferred directly from, say, the word processor (a stripped-down version of *Apple Writer*) to the database manager (a version of *Quick File*). To transfer data, move a word processor file to the package's clipboard, and then move it to a database file (there are not pull-down windows). This type of integration may not be the best—compared to some other systems reviewed in this chapter, it is primitive—but it operates within the range of tolerance of most libraries.

AppleWorks also supports ASCII (text) files, DIF (Data Interchange Format), and files from Apple's *Quick File*. Another good feature is its standardized structure: it is not necessary to learn separate sets of commands for each module, though some components have more commands than others (all are easy to use). The database system is only marginally flexible, allowing, for instance, only 20 characters per field and short record length. The capacity of all these components depends upon the RAM storage of the microcomputer.

Review sources:	*Nibble Magazine*, December 1989, 34.
	The Computing Teacher, December/January 1990, 36.
Related programs:	*ReportWorks, ThinkWorks, MegaWorks, SpellWorks, OfficeWorks, LibraryWorks*. Templates for library use available through several sources.
Documentation:	Excellent large manual. Help screen. Disk tutorial, sample files. Additional materials are available from many publishers.

Name:	**AppleWorks GS**
Program type:	Integrated software
Vendor:	Claris Corporation
Cost:	$299
Hardware requirements:	Apple IIGS
Description:	Similar to *AppleWorks*, above, but much more powerful, taking advantage of the superior technology of the hardware. For many IIGS users, this may be the major program that will satisfy most of their office needs. Six applications are included: word processing, spreadsheet, database management, mail merge, page layout, and graphics. The word processor contains an excellent spell checker and a thesaurus with 470,000 words. The window system allows up to 14 files to be active at one time and the user may move among them. The package's problems involve the hardware; on a lesser equipped GS the system will operate more sluggishly

than many people would like. Otherwise, *AppleWorks GS* is an outstanding purchase.

Review sources: *The Computing Teacher*, May 1989, 43.
Home-Office Computing, October 1989, 78.

Related programs: *OfficeWorks*, and other template packages listed in this volume

Documentation: Excellent and easy-to-use 300-page reference manual and a separate start-up and installation manual offer a step-by-step guide to using each component of the system. Quick Reference Card included.

Name: **DESQView**
Program type: Software integrator
Vendor: Quarterdeck Office Systems
Cost: $129.95
Hardware requirements: IBM and compatibles
Description: System provides for integrated software management of normally separate programs. The program allows a spreadsheet to be used within a word processor or other program without rebooting the computer. The program is also very good at memory management. Compatible with many 386 processor programs, the program is very useful for people who need to run a wide range of programs conveniently.
Review sources: *InfoWorld*, February 13, 1989, 51.
Computer Shopper, January 1989, 363.
Documentation: Manual of over 200 pages provides instructions for installation, programming, and operation. Easy to read, with index.

Name: **Framework III**
Program type: Integrated software
Vendor: Ashton-Tate
Cost: $695
Hardware requirements: IBM and compatibles, hard-disk drive recommended, mouse optional
Description: Powerful system integrates eight separate functions: word processing (including thesaurus and spell checker), spreadsheet, database management, outlining, graphics, telecommunications, electronic mail, and local area network support. Modules work together very well, making transfer of data simple. Commands are identical among components, shortening the learning curve for such a powerful system. *dBase* files can be imported without any special problems.

A new version, *Framework III LAN*, is designed to run on local area networks. It is available separately for $995.

Review sources: *Computer Shopper*, March 1989, 356.

Computer Shopper, June 1989, 363.

Documentation: Three manuals provide tutorial, procedures, FRED programming language help, and references to all sections mentioned above

Name: **Lotus 1-2-3**

Program type: Integrated software

Vendor: Lotus Development Corporation

Cost: $595

Hardware requirements: IBM and compatibles

Description: The first great integrated software produced, this package has no word processor, but contains spreadsheet, database management, and graphics. *1-2-3* has been extremely popular as a high-level business system. New version contains many improvements, including the ability to install it on a local area network.

Most popular in the system is the spreadsheet; all other components are subordinate to it and unable to function without it. For example, the information manager component (not database manager), using essentially the same grid, uses data from the spreadsheet; the graphics system captures and also uses data from the spreadsheet.

The system comes with a six-lesson tutorial that covers all major functions, making start-up uncomplicated even for novices. Computation and recalculation of this assembly-language program are fast, and there is extensive online help. *1-2-3* has five basic charts: bar, stacked bar, side-by-side bar, pie, and scatter. They are created with simple keystrokes, a great advantage over earlier and less sophisticated spreadsheets, such as *VisiCalc*. Essentially, all operation modes may be carried out with same command structure.

Symphony, an upgraded version of *1-2-3*, adds telecommunications, word processing, a more potent database, and window management system. For business spreadsheet users, either system is an excellent and safe choice.

Review sources: *PC Magazine*, November 28, 1989, 197.

Personal Computing, November 1989, 143.

Documentation: Manual contains over 350 pages of in-depth coverage of many areas. Other books also cover both *1-2-3* and *Sym-*

phony, and users may wish to consult them, both before and after purchase.

Name:	**Microsoft Works**
Program type:	Integrated software
Vendor:	Microsoft
Cost:	$295
Hardware requirements:	Macintosh
Description:	This very capable and perhaps best integrated program for the Macintosh contains word processor, spreadsheet, and database management system. Pull-down menus are used to good effect, helping the neophyte. Advanced users may use direct command sequences. All components of the system share data by cutting and pasting among up to fourteen documents that may be open on the desktop at one time. Special feature allows saving mouse keyclicks as a macro command.

Word-processing module supports footers and headers, and mail merge, and it comes with a good spell checker.

The spreadsheet's capacity is 256 columns by at least 16,832 rows. It will display statistics with bar charts, pie charts, and quadratic charts. Chart utility can be used within the spreadsheet without the need to exit and reenter.

Database component is not relational, but it does support custom data entry screens, label production, and restructuring as needed.

The package's marginal communications component should not be mistaken for a more sophisticated program. However, the system will support file transfers with XMODEM.

Overall, this excellent system is reasonably priced and easy to use.

Review sources:	*MacWorld*, April 1989, 165.
	Macuser, April 1989, 150.
Documentation:	Instruction manual provides detailed start-up, installation, and reference material

Name:	**PFS: First Choice**
Program type:	Integrated software
Vendor:	Software Publishing Corporation
Cost:	$149
Hardware requirements:	IBM and compatibles

Description: This package evolved from the software put out by PFS for many years. Separate functions have been integrated into a single package, including spreadsheet, word processor, database manager, and telecommunications. It is an excellent package for the average user. It will not satisfy the needs of advanced users or those who need graphics, yet it provides an excellent package with many features. It is also much easier to learn than packages that may contain more features than needed.

Limitations are apparent in the word processor. The system will handle documents only a few dozen pages in length. The database system will handle up to 16,000 records and an unlimited number of fields, dependent upon the size of disk drive. Printouts from the database module are predetermined and limited. The spreadsheet will handle 255 rows by 70 columns.

One serious defect of the package is its inability to export or import data to or from other software packages, except for the word processor function which can use ASCII files.

Review sources: *Library Software Review*, November–December 1987, 397. *PC World*, February 1989, 86.

Documentation: Printed tutorial, tear-out reference card, and excellent manual. With its ease of use, program does not require much documentation.

Interlibrary Loan

In the first version of this book, only one interlibrary loan system was listed: FILLS. Now there are several. They help to automate two basic interlibrary loan functions: generating request forms and transmitting the data to a network or microcomputer bulletin board system using the electronic mail functions. FILLS can perform both of these functions well. Electronic bulletin board systems are described elsewhere.

Name:	**Bookpath**
Program type:	Interlibrary loan subsystem
Vendor:	Alpine Data, Inc.
Cost:	$595
Hardware requirements:	IBM and compatibles, 10-megabyte hard-disk drive
Description:	System can be used to track ILL of books as well as magazines and newspapers with standard ILL forms. Provides a database of patrons and library requests and can be searched by author, title, subject, library or date, with Boolean operators. Reports can be generated using the same criteria.

Name:	**FILLS** (Fast Inter Library Loans and Statistics)
Program type:	Interlibrary loan
Vendor:	MacNeal Hospital
Cost:	$360, licensed for use on one microcomputer only; $495, including OnTyme software
Hardware requirements:	IBM and compatibles
Description:	Reports indicate that this menu-driven program reduces the work by 40 to 60 percent in preparing special pinfed ALA interlibrary forms. FILLS may be used with OnTyme to send requests, since it will not send requests by itself (documentation has a chapter on using other telecommunications software, such as *Smartcom, PC Talk*, and *Crosstalk*). FILLS generates statistical reports, including time between

original entry and final disposition, total cost, libraries from which materials were borrowed, and frequency of borrowed materials. The FILLS form is displayed on screen and filled in by user. Great advantage of this program is that subsequent requests from a library for a title can be answered by recalling information from a stored request by number; data will be filled in by FILLS. Several reports are available: alphabetical periodical title lists, alphabetical library address lists, total cost charged per periodical title, number of requests per library, average return time per library, percentage fill rate per library, total and average costs charged per library, outstanding loan reports by both patron name and date range, number of requests by department, and numerical department lists.

Even after all information has been entered, data can be changed before saving the loan for printing purposes. Requests may be printed and sent via electronic mail, or printed and sent to a file for later electronic mail transmission as part of a batch. Program reports when a particular file is nearly full, and report program must be run to clear it. Once transmitted, requests may be deleted from the system. Capacity for outstanding loans is 400 on double-sided disk, or 2000 with IBM XT or AT; it is important to record returned loans regularly to free up disk space. Loans may be sent to another library, filled, or cancelled. Mailing labels may be generated.

Program produces special lists: alphabetical periodical list of all titles library has requested (periodical title information for up to 1000 periodicals per double-sided disk, or 3200 on XT, is saved, and each request is given a number. Subsequent requests may be entered with code number); addresses of all libraries borrowed from; and numerical list of departments (15 spaces each) for which interlibrary loan requests have been made.

Installation is relatively easy. Users of version 1.0 must recreate library and periodical files (neither time consuming nor difficult).

Review sources: Williams, Delmas E. "Software Reviews; F.I.L.L.S.," *Technical Services Quarterly*, Winter 1986, 89–92.

Documentation: Excellent manual with extensive and easy-to-follow instructions for installation and procedures. Complete walkthrough for entire system. Contains sample FILLS-generated reports.

Name:	**ILL Patron Request System**
Program type:	Interlibrary loan
Vendor:	Harold B. Lee Library
Cost:	$500 (inquire about discount available); demonstration available
Hardware requirements:	IBM and compatibles with 10 megabyte hard-disk drive, Epson compatible printer.
Description:	System was developed by the Harold B. Lee Library Interlibrary Loan Department (Brigham Young University) and has been in use since 1986. System creates record of each request. Subsequent actions, such as ordered, received, returned, are maintained as record is updated. Functions include: status reports, receive, return, update records with OCLC SaveScreen data, writes OCLC Micro Enhancer data, generates ALA requests, prepares overdue and cancellation letters, billing procedures, statistical reports, and more.

Name:	**Interlibrary Loan Control**
Program type:	Interlibrary loan
Vendor:	Right On Programs
Cost:	$149
Hardware requirements:	IBM and compatibles
Description:	Uses forms based on ALA standard. Menu-driven program allows easy entry of data, with space for custom message, such as ''Fill at no cost only,'' borrower's name, etc. Request mode will make, edit, delete, or display a request. Loan mode will do the same for a loan. A number of reports and printouts are possible: yearly statistics, condensed listing, check-in log, check-out log.
Documentation:	Simple booklet

Name:	**OCLC ILL Micro Enhancer**
Program type:	Interlibrary loan subsystem
Vendor:	OCLC
Cost:	Contact vendor for current pricing
Hardware requirements:	OCLC M-300
Description:	System provides enhancement for OCLC basic interlibrary loan subsystem. System will dial out and log on to the OCLC online system and batch process automatically once time has been set by user. Frees staff from routine, repetitive chores.

Inventory Control

Aside from the full circulation and integrated packages listed elsewhere in this volume, there are no software packages that will take an inventory of all books in the library. The packages listed below help in the simple inventory and tracking of special collections such as musical instruments, audiovisual equipment, supplies, etc.

Name:	**Equipment Inventory Control**
Program type:	Inventory control
Vendor:	Right On Programs
Cost:	$119, IBM; $99, Apple
Hardware requirements:	IBM and compatibles; Apple II series
Description:	Data about any type of equipment may be entered into this simple database: VCR, typewriter, TVs, pencils—even software. Fields are titled model number, serial number, name, material type, location and condition. Each field may then be searched. Menu selection makes it easy to examine all of the items in the database, or to print out a listing of all items. Combinations of fields can also be selected to pull out additional useful information. According to the vendor, the crew of an ocean liner uses this program to keep track of all of the tools on board the ship.
Documentation:	Simple booklet

Name:	**Musical Instrument Inventory Control**
Program type:	Inventory control
Vendor:	Right On Programs
Cost:	$89
Hardware requirements:	IBM and compatibles; Apple II series
Description:	This simple program for keeping track of musical instruments is for schools needing to keep track of instruments on loan or rented to students. Database stores information about

119

manufacturer, condition, cost in dollars, user, model number, serial number, location, and purchase date for each instrument. Information can be recalled to screen or sent to printer by instrument, serial number, location, or condition. All information can be displayed or printed by serial number or instrument. This program is perfect for people who need to maintain this type of database and who have few other uses for their computer.

Documentation: Simple booklet

Name: **Sheet Music Inventory Control**
Program type: Inventory control
Vendor: Right On Programs
Cost: $89
Hardware requirements: IBM and compatibles; Apple II series
Description: Some libraries have extensive sheet music collections that can be difficult to control or access. With this easy-to-use program, keeping track of a collection and making it accessible to patrons is a much simpler task. Sheet music is first entered into the system using the fields: number of copies, rating, publisher, title, category, part, group, cost, and date. Search is possible only on title, category, part or group. Lists may be sent to screen or printer. This is a really good, easy to use database for sheet music management.

Documentation: Simple booklet

Name: **Supplies Inventory Control**
Program type: Inventory control
Vendor: Right On Programs
Cost: $119
Hardware requirements: IBM and compatibles; Apple II series
Description: This simple database program allows any size of library to keep track of supplies. Materials such as pencils, paper, and ribbons can be assigned an identification number and entered by name, color, and cost. When the list is complete, an order report can be generated. Materials are checked in as they arrive. Requested items are deleted, forming the basis for a new order. Reports from this system can easily help staff to determine the rate at which supplies are ordered to ensure that overordering does not take place. Database may be edited and searched as needed. Supplier list can be printed in either condensed version or with items attached.

Documentation: Simple booklet

Name:	**Textbook Inventory Control**
Program type:	Inventory control
Vendor:	Right On Programs
Cost:	$99
Hardware requirements:	IBM and compatibles
Description:	Schools often need to track the number of textbooks available for each class and to loan and retrieve them on a semester basis. Program keeps record of books owned, and makes inventory and collection maintenance a much easier job. Main menu provides selection for data entry of names of textbooks, plus cost, publisher, edition, grade level, etc. Teachers and the grades and subjects they teach are also entered. Assignment of books is also simple. Reports include student, teachers, and textbooks.
Documentation:	Simple booklet is all that is required.

Local Area Networks

Local area networks (LANs) provide a link among several microcomputers. Users can exchange electronic mail and data, and can share expensive equipment such as a laser printer. LAN users in the same building (or cluster of buildings) have immediate access to all other users in the network. Networking occurs when two or more micros are used to circulate and share the same patron data. LANs are also used when librarians wish to link staff on different floors or areas. In most local area networks, no modems are required. Instead, the computers are "hardwired" with a cable directly to each other, making a permanent link.

One drawback of LANs is that they are complicated and expensive. Some systems also require that a microcomputer be dedicated to running the system. Over the years, the technology has become less expensive and less difficult to manage, but it still remains the province of consultants and technicians.

Name:	**LANtastic**
Program type:	Local area network
Vendor:	Artisoft, Inc.
Cost:	$99 per node
Hardware requirements:	Macintosh; IBM and compatibles
Description:	Easy system to install. Allows printer sharing, backup routines, electronic mail, and CD-ROM sharing. Menu-driven system can be installed without onsite consultant or vendor. Also has low memory overhead requirement. Server requires only 40K. Workstations require only 10K. Stations connected by regular phone wire.

Name:	**Plus Link**
Program type:	Local area network for circulation system
Vendor:	Follett Software Company
Cost:	$277, host hardware; $498, terminal set required for each station; cables also available at various prices.
Hardware requirements:	IBM and compatibles

Description: For libraries that use *Circulation Plus* or have considered using it, this option makes it possible to spread the system throughout a building and yet have all terminals linked. Using special hardware and software, *Plus Link* allows libraries to check materials out from any networked terminal. Contact vendor for additional and more detailed information.

Related programs: Designed to work with *Circulation Plus*, *Textbook Plus*, and *Catalog Plus*

Documentation: Network manual

Name: **Winnebago LAN**

Program type: Local area network

Vendor: Winnebago

Cost: Contact vendor for current pricing

Hardware requirements: IBM and compatibles with hard-disk drive and 2 megabytes for each 1000 items in database

Description: System allows library to network different workstations for card catalog or circulation system. Two or more IBM PCs will work together. System uses standard Ethernet network and will transfer at the rate of 10 megabits per second. Access restrictions may be imposed on use of information contained in files.

Miscellaneous Programs

Some software packages just do not fall neatly into any of the other categories in this book, so they appear together here under the heading of "miscellaneous." Some of these programs are enhancements to other programs, some are template sets, and some, such as *OrgPlus*, are one of a kind in this volume.

Name:	**MegaWorks**
Program type:	*AppleWorks* enhancement
Vendor:	Megahaus
Cost:	$49.95
Hardware requirements:	Apple II series
Description:	*MegaWorks* adds a spell checker to *AppleWorks*. A word dictionary of 40,000 words checks for misspelled and suspicious spellings. Up to 10,000 words may be added by the user to customize the dictionary. This module also adds mail merge. Personalized form letters may be created using *AppleWorks* and then merged with database files.
Related programs:	*AppleWorks; ThinkWorks; ReportWorks*

Name:	**OrgPlus Advanced 5.0**
Program type:	Organization chart
Vendor:	Banner Blue
Cost:	$100
Hardware requirements:	IBM and compatibles
Description:	For any organization large enough to periodically draft and regularly update an organization chart, this program will be useful. Charts may be printed in a variety of included fonts, including those for a LaserJet or compatible printer. Program permits drawing both vertical and horizontal lines and windows, sideways printing, block manipulation, bold, italic, and underline. Margins are easily changed. Sixteen different styles of charts are supported, making chart crea-

tion quick and easy. Charts can also be previewed onscreen prior to actual printing. Additional reports, such as a phone list, can be printed in up to four columns. Contains many useful features.

Name:	**Report Works**
Program type:	*AppleWorks* enhancement
Vendor:	Megahaus
Cost:	$49.95
Hardware requirements:	Apple II series
Description:	This program will improve the capability of *AppleWorks* by providing several new features to standard functions. Forms can be formatted onscreen to facilitate design. The program makes it easy to create full-page forms for purchase orders, statements, invoices, overdues, etc. Math functions allow users to calculate in the database and word processing modes. Information in the database and spreadsheet files can be sorted on several levels. Information from several files can be combined and headings added. A very important accessory to *AppleWorks*, it is easy to use and worth the investment for most users.
Related programs:	*AppleWorks; MegaWorks; ThinkWorks*
Documentation:	Unknown

Name:	**Schedule Master**
Program type:	Employee schedule
Vendor:	Schedule Master Corporation
Cost:	$1,995
Hardware requirements:	IBM and compatibles with hard-disk drive
Description:	This expensive schedule program will create very detailed, ongoing schedules for many employees. Basic information about each employee is entered into the database first. Each employee may be coded in up to 26 different ways for tasks. Considerable flexibility is allowed in this program. Both the number of hours that the employee can work in a day and the number that they are willing to work may be entered.
Review sources:	''Scheduling Software for MS-DOS Microcomputers,'' *Computers In Libraries*, January–February 1991, 41.
Documentation:	Manual does not contain screenshots and is less than useful. However, program itself contains many help features.

Name:	**SchoolWorks: Letter Files**
Program type:	Template set for *AppleWorks* or *Microsoft Works*

Vendor:	K–12 MicroMedia
Cost:	$55
Hardware requirements:	Apple II series, with *AppleWorks*; IBM and compatibles with *Microsoft Works*
Description:	Contains over 40 letter templates ready for loading into the computer, altering, and printing. Can be used by staff and by the general public on a public access microcomputer. Some of the administrator letters are announcing award, faculty death, fire alarms, open house, job refusal, LD testing, scholarship program, phone use. Letters for a teacher include book review, field trip, scholarship recommendation, teacher award recommendation. Other letters for use by a guidance counselor and athletic staff are included. Mail merge letters also included.

Name:	**SchoolWorks: Media Center**
Program type:	Template package for word processing, database, and spreadsheet
Vendor:	K–12 MicroMedia
Cost:	$55
Hardware requirements:	Apple II series with AppleWorks; IBM and compatibles with *Microsoft Works*
Description:	Excellent template package, reasonably priced, helps prepare bibliographies, budgets, catalog cards, periodical management, reserves, and acquisitions. This template package provides dozens of applications for use with the database, spreadsheet, and word processor. Not all libraries can make use of all of the templates, but most are sure to find more than enough to make it a worthwhile purchase. All can be altered for a particular library. Other files include: staff schedules, video schedules, gradebook, volunteer skills chart, daily circulation, lesson plans, form letter request for freebies, and many more. Perfect for the very small library with limited access to other programs and technology.
Review sources:	*Booklist*, December 1, 1988, 662. *Apple Library User Group Newsletter*, July 1990, 73.
Related programs:	*SchoolWorks: Athletic Director*; *SchoolWorks: Teacher*; *SchoolWorks: Office*; *SchoolWorks: Letter Files*; *ThinkWorks*.
Documentation:	Excellent manual of instructions

Name:	**SideKick Plus**
Program type:	Desktop accessory

Vendor:	Borland
Cost:	$199.95
Hardware requirements:	IBM and compatibles, with hard-disk drive
Description:	This easy-to-use program has a number of quick and useful functions. It emulates many of the items we use on our desk every day: calendar/appointment book, notepad, calculator, dialer—and works very well indeed. A directory of phone numbers, with names and addresses, may be created as a dialer for voice communications (sample directory comes with system); position the cursor line on a name and the program will dial the number. The notepad is a word processor with unusual abilities: notes can be typed in for future reference, and the notepad will save whatever is on the screen. The user does not need to leave a program to do this, simply to pause while the data is saved to disk. This feature is particularly helpful for word processing, where charts or other material can be put into documents. In this sense, *SideKick Plus* is an integrator and a desktop publishing accessory; it makes a number of programs compatible.

The appointment and calendar function appears to have no limit. It can accommodate dates beyond the year 2000, for people who truly plan ahead. A month-by-month calendar appears on screen, and a particular date is highlighted for appointment entry from 8 a.m. to 9 p.m. at half-hour intervals. Two other handy features are a pop-up ASCII table and import and export data ability.

Review sources:	*PC Resource*, October 1988, 742. *Compute!*, December 1988, 89.
Related programs:	*SideKick for Presentation Managers* is a similar system for use with desktop publishing programs.
Documentation:	A 122-page manual of clear, concise instructions and examples

Name:	**SurveyWorks**
Program type:	Survey management system
Vendor:	K–12 MicroMedia
Cost:	$195
Hardware requirements:	Apple II series; Scantron Scanner
Description:	Allows for the creation of a survey of up to 90 questions. Each question can be coded with five possible responses. Answers are put directly onto the test paper, which is then scanned by the computer and put into an ASCII file for analysis. Results include a simple frequency distribution

and the option of a count of responses. Menu-driven setup. May also be used with *AppleWorks* and data merged into a spreadsheet file for further statistical analysis.

Name:	**ThinkWorks**
Program type:	Outline processing for word processing module of *AppleWorks*
Vendor:	K–12 MicroMedia
Cost:	$49.95
Hardware requirements:	Apple II series
Description:	For the writing of reports, proposals, or longer documents, this is a useful tool that allows users to create outlines of their ideas with up to ten levels of entries. Outlines may be merged and saved in *AppleWorks* format with or without tab stops.
Related programs:	*AppleWorks*; *ReportWorks*; *MegaWorks*

Name:	**Windows**
Program type:	Operating system
Vendor:	Microsoft
Cost:	Contact vendor for current pricing
Hardware requirements:	IBM and compatibles
Description:	This program simulates the easy command format of the Macintosh computer for IBM computers. Pull-down menus and a mouse are supported, making a Macintosh user feel right at home. Many programs are already incorporated into the system, but users may find some a bit difficult to get to work correctly. The latest version of this system has apparently eliminated many bugs of the first. A worthwhile program, especially for use with microcomputers with large RAM and a hard-disk drive.

The system virtually eliminates direct interaction with DOS. Files can be opened, closed, or moved. A special desktop area allows for notepad, calendar, clock, a terminal communications program, a card file, and more.

Working with the large and often unwieldy directories of a hard-disk drive is made simple and fast with pull-down menus and the mouse.

Windows Write, a word-processing program, is included. Users may create documents as well as cut and paste material, including graphics, from other applications such as *Multiplan*, *Lotus 1-2-3*, and *Windows Paint*.

Review sources:	*Library Software Review*, March–April, 1991, 120.

Documentation: Excellent manuals for writing program, the windows operating environment, and desktop applications provide easy-to-follow instruction.

Online Catalog

Creating an online catalog to speed access to the library's materials can take a long time. Some of the systems below facilitate this process. One sets up an AV catalog; the other two handle larger systems. All have an online catalog system as their main function. Other more integrated systems, which can be used to perform many different library functions, are found elsewhere in this book.

Important considerations in choosing an online catalog program are capacity and the amount of integration with other library activities, such as cataloging and circulation, that is required. If you need an integrated library system, look in the section on integrated library systems.

Name:	**Circulation/Catalog Plus**
Program type:	Circulation and online public access catalog
Vendor:	Follett Software
Cost:	$3,190. Toll-free number support for one year, with free updates and upgrades. Subsequent support available, $275 per site, per year.
Hardware requirements:	IBM and compatibles, 3 megabytes extended memory, 30 or more megabyte hard-disk drive with minimum of 30 milliseconds access time. Streaming tape backup suggested.
Description:	Provides for both circulation system and online public access catalog. System is integrated and MARC compatible. Program provides for 28 reports and lists, inventory, status of items, reserve report, and statistics.
Related programs:	*Catalog Plus*

Name:	**On-Line Catalog**
Program type:	Online catalog
Vendor:	Right On Programs
Cost:	$249
Hardware requirements:	IBM and compatibles; Macintosh

130

Description: This online catalog program is excellent for the smaller library. Books may be entered with ease. A system management menu allows for editing and deleting books once entered, as well as for a printout of an alphabetical list of subjects and shelflist cards. Password protected. Catalog data may include ISBN, accession number, price, LC number, and location. A complete printout by subject is available to patron or librarian by simply pressing "P." Patrons may search by title, author, and up to six subject headings. Five of the "hits" or titles are displayed at one time on the screen. The information appears in catalog card format on the screen. The exact number of entries allowed is determined by the disk space available. The program can handle approximately 1000 entries per megabyte.

Name: **On-Line Plus**

Program type: Online catalog

Vendor: Right On Programs

Cost: $249

Hardware requirements: IBM and compatibles; Macintosh; hard disk

Description: This program has full features of *On-Line Catalog*, above, plus the catalog card production package, *Catalog Carder*. Can be used with a bar code wand if desired.

Related programs: *On-Line Catalog*; *Catalog Carder*

Documentation: Easy-to-follow simple instructions

Project Management

Project management programs are available for most types of microcomputers. They can help track materials and personnel, and aid in scheduling. They are obviously more useful for the very large library that has larger, more complicated projects with which to contend.

Such packages are useful for adding up all of the various components involved and arriving at a final estimate of costs. They are also good for helping the librarian to think through a cost structure in an organized manner, making it less likely that something important will be forgotten.

It can also be useful to have computer-assisted conclusions to convince the library board.

Name:	**InstaPlan 5000**
Program type:	Project management package
Vendor:	InstaPlan Corporation
Cost:	$495
Hardware requirements:	IBM and compatibles
Description:	A feature-packed program for project management helps users to identify, sequence, and schedule projects by task and activities. *InstaPlan* makes it easy to organize and outline a project, assign resources including people and material, and project a cost. Excellent program for larger libraries.
Review sources:	*Library Software Review*, November–December 1990, 404.
Documentation:	Excellent manual. Includes screenshots, keyboard template, and good instructions.

Public Access

Public access microcomputers were popular before microcomputers became commonplace in libraries for staff work. The problems with public access computers' use, upkeep and maintenance are very different, since they are being used by many people. Much software may be needed, compared with only a few packages required for library staff work.

Providing public access computers can require a lot of different services, including walk-in, circulation of hardware and software, electronic bulletin boards, and much more.

Some of the rules that will assist in making a public access computer site more successful include the following:

Make appointments for users.
Appointments should last for one hour.
Select a wide range of software for use at a public access site.

Only a small example of software is listed in this section. It includes educational programs (especially library skills), reading referral or encouragement programs, and entertainment and utility programs.

Name:	**Bookmate**
Program type:	Reading referral
Vendor:	Sunburst Communications
Cost:	$65; lab pack of ten, $195; Corvus Network, $260; AppleTalk Network, $260
Hardware requirements:	Apple II series
Description:	*Bookmate* is a set of four programs that provide reading referral to students for grades 3–6. Three hundred books by popular authors are used in the program, and the librarian can include books that are actually in the library. The program is extremely simple to use; students will have little difficulty. Each module is geared to helping students select books in a different way. Mind Reader is a selection tool

aimed at determining a student's mood. Calendar Trivia will select a book based on a date of the year. Time Machine picks reading based on history, from 1706 to 2500. A "time machine" appears on the screen and users adjust it to the year in which they are interested. After using the simple menu selection process, one to three book suggestions will be displayed. A description of each is available. Students can also use the module Studio One to select books that have been made into movies and to take on the role of movie producer. They decide type of action, type of main character, and location, and one to three books appear on the screen that meet these criteria. The information can also be printed out. Responses are personalized with student's name. All in all, a colorful and imaginative way for students to be assisted by the computer in selecting books for reading.

Documentation: Excellent 50-page manual with instructions, suggestions, list of books, and bibliography

Name: **How to Write for Everyday Living**
Program type: Writing improvement
Vendor: Educational Activities, Inc.
Cost: $159
Hardware requirements: Apple II series
Description: This is an excellent example of a good public access package. Program exercises are structured around real life situations: fill out an application to obtain a driver's license, fill out deposit and withdrawal slips for savings accounts, wrestle with checkbook, write a resume, organize information into lists and outlines, write business and personal letters, etc. Can be used by young people in grades 4–12 as well as by adults, especially those who are new to the United States.
Documentation: A 26-page notebook of instructions and samples of various job-application forms

Name: **Public Domain Software on File (Apple)**
Program type: Public domain software
Vendor: Facts On File
Cost: $195
Hardware requirements: Apple II series
Description: Librarians often ask about software that can be circulated to patrons without fear of copyright infringement. One form is public domain software. Unfortunately, much public do-

main software has errors. Facts on File has solved this problem by debugging several hundred popular programs, organizing them into useful categories (e.g., entertainment, business, home, etc.), and packaging them attractively. The resulting package can be used in the library or at home by patrons to make their own copies. Twenty-two diskettes contain over 200 programs.

Review sources: *Choice*, July–August 1986, 1744.
Wilson Library Bulletin, December 1985, 59.

Related programs: *Public Domain Software on File (IBM)* and *Public Domain Software on File Collection on CD-ROM*.

Documentation: 32-page booklet

Name: **Public Domain Software on File (IBM)**
Program type: Public domain software
Vendor: Facts On File
Cost: $195, basic set; $50, satellite set
Hardware requirements: IBM and compatibles
Description: Set of 12 core and 4 satellite disks contains over 150 ready-to-use programs covering many useful areas. Many may be used by librarians for inhouse work, while all may be copied by patrons to take home. Word processing, database management, telecommunications, utilities, home management, adult and child education, and programming languages are some of the broad categories into which the programs have been grouped.

Review sources: *Wilson Library Bulletin*, October 1989, 87.
Related programs: *Public Domain Software on File (Apple)*, and *Public Domain Software on File Collection on CD-ROM*.
Documentation: 32-page booklet

Name: **Reading in the Workplace**
Program type: Reading improvement for adults
Vendor: Educational Activities, Inc.
Cost: $295, for complete set; $119, for any of three reading levels (Grades 3–5, 5–7, and 7–9). Backup disks provided.
Hardware requirements: Apple II series
Description: High-interest topics related to actual workplace situation. Designed to help adult workers read and understand job-related materials such as manuals, technical materials, and written directions. It focuses on vocabulary improvement, contextual analysis, and comprehension skills. Each of three available units has 16 stories that deal with main

idea, details, inference and conclusion, and vocabulary. Jobs included are roofing a house, pouring concrete, wiring, general contracting, patching plaster, and insulation.

Documentation: Manual of instructions, management system, and reproducible activity masters

Reference and Reference Statistics

Many of the programs in the database management, spreadsheet, and word processing sections of this book can be pressed into service for use at the reference desk. Those described below have been specifically designed to aid in reference work, either keeping track of materials in a ready-reference collection or handling output measure data collection and evaluation.

Name:	**Create: A Reference Statistics Program**
Program type:	Reference statistics
Vendor:	MecklerSoft
Cost:	$59.95
Hardware requirements:	IBM and compatibles; Apple II series
Description:	With this "authoring" system, user creates customized database management program for statistical reports and tallies, as well as analyses of survey material. Its use is straightforward, but it is not without some occasional problem. Users must have an initialized disk, and once the program has been created, it is independent of master disk. Users choose from 80 predetermined fields or select new fields of their choice. Typical data that program will track include day of week and time, length of transaction, type of location, name of person who took survey, reference sources or books, subject category, and whether survey was made by phone, in person, or by mail. Surveys may be completed on paper, then input into program for analysis. It is easy to "bomb" the program, however—at least before operation is mastered. Some input instructions are not immediately clear, but this is a minor complaint and does not interfere with overall utility of program. Statistics in all fields may be generated as a two-dimensional frequency table.

Review sources:	Smith, Dana E., "Customized Reference Statistics Programs," *American Libraries*, March 1984, 179.
	Library Software Review, November–December, 1988, 425.
Documentation:	Booklet has hints on sampling techniques and many forms to help design *Create* programs.

Name:	**OutputM** (version 2.0)
Program type:	Output measure statistics
Vendor:	Center for the Study of Rural Librarianship (program funded by LSCA and developed with Library Development Division, State of Pennsylvania)
Cost:	$99
Hardware requirements:	IBM and compatibles
Description:	The program's basic function is to automate tabulation of 21 library transactions for the collection of output measures: annual circulation, annual in-library material use, annual library visits, annual reference transactions, annual program attendance, holdings, library registrations, number of browsers, browsers finding something, number of reference transactions, reference transactions completed, subjects and authors found, subjects and authors sought, number of titles sought, population—legal service area, requests immediately unavailable, requests available in 7 days, requests available in 14 days, requests available in 30 days, and requests available in more than 30 days. Designed for all types and sizes of library, program can handle data for five districts, each with 50 member libraries, or 250 total. Data may be cumulated for one year only, but stored for ten years. Statistical calculations include average data for one or all libraries.
	A sample file facilitates learning the program. From main menu, users may create a new file, assign names to districts or libraries, enter or examine library data, summarize, or exit. Summarizing feature produces either total or average amounts for 20 of the above transactions and services.
Review sources:	"*OutputM* Simplifies Output Measures Record Keeping," *American Libraries*, December 1984, 830.
Documentation:	A 20-page accompanying document covers starting a sample file, and backing up disks. Installation procedures for hard or floppy disk are clearly outlined.

Name:	**Reference and Information Station Program**
Program type:	Reference database

Vendor: MecklerSoft
Cost: $59.95
Hardware requirements: Apple II series; IBM and compatibles
Description: This program provides public access reference and directional question assistance. Program allows library staff to format screens and menus according to needs. Patron then accesses directional, reference, or policy matters by menu selections. A statistical subroutine will track user interaction.

Retrospective Conversion

One of the least envied jobs in the library is that of retrospective conversion, often to MARC format. With the entire MARC database now available on CD-ROM, it is much easier for a library, even a small one, to take advantage of the microcomputer for this function.

Name:	**Alliance Plus**
Program type:	Retrospective conversion CD-ROM MARC database
Vendor:	Follett Software
Cost:	$950; $450 for renewal
Hardware requirements:	IBM and compatibles, 20-megabyte hard-disk drive, Hitachi 3600 CD-ROM drive with card and cable (internal or external)
Description:	Requires *Circulation/Catalog Plus*, and *Plus Link*. Database contains more than 300,000 book, AV, serial, and juvenile records. Allows library to perform own shelflist retrospective conversion. Quarterly updates by subscription will continue to provide support for new titles. Has direct interface with *Circulation/Catalog Plus*. Aimed specifically at school libraries, the product can be helpful to any small library.
	Two search modes, menu-driven or advanced, can be used with fields ISBN, LCCN, ISSN, title, author, subject, and series. Allows for full or truncated search and delimiters of material type, year ranges, readability levels, and interest levels. Materials found in the CD-ROM catalog are taken directly into *Circulation/Catalog Plus* for editing, etc.
	A great tool for collection development and catalog building.
Name:	**Bib-Base/MARC**
Program type:	MARC cataloging
Vendor:	Small Library Computing, Inc.

Cost: $495; demonstration disk and manual, $20

Hardware requirements: IBM and compatibles

Description: Add-on module provides for loading full MARC records into *Bib-Base*, as well as editing and outputing these records.

Related programs: *Bib-Base/Acq* and *Bib-Base/Cat*

Name: **BiblioFile Catalog Production System**

Program type: Retrospective conversion

Vendor: Library Corporation

Cost: $2,930, CD-ROM drive, *BiblioFile* access and application software, support and maintenance for one year; $870, one-year subscription to LC MARC, English-language; additional fees and services available: inquire

Hardware requirements: IBM and compatibles (CD-ROM supplied)

Description: Provides access to over 3 million MARC records on four laser disks. Gives in-house access to Library of Congress English and foreign-language MARC bibliographic records. The four CD-ROM disks are periodically recompiled and reissued, and system comes with CD-ROM player to attach to user-supplied computer. Functions include searching the database, editing MARC records, creating original MARC records, displaying catalog card image, saving edited records, transmitting directly to another computer system, printing cards and labels locally, and converting to OCLC-type magnetic tape.

Up to 99 titles may be recalled per search, and search may be made by any word in title, author's name, ISBN, or LCCN. Items may be saved to disk, which may be searched later to review work. Printer options allow for customized cards. Program will also print spine or book pocket labels. Help windows are available at any time and easy to summon and use.

Program was used successfully to expedite retrospective conversion by Phillips Memorial Library of Providence College (see citation below), which has 250,000 volumes. 10,000 volumes were converted to machine-readable form. If a MARC record was found in *BiblioFile* database, it was stored on a floppy disk for later editing and, ultimately, stored in library's catalog.

Review sources: Desmarais, Norman, ''BiblioFile,'' *Library Software Review*, January–February 1986, 28.

Desmarais, Norman, "BiblioFile for Retrospective Conversion," *Small Computers in Libraries*, December 1985, 24.

Related programs: The Library Corporation also makes available *BiblioFile Circulation*, *BiblioFile Intelligent Catalog*, and *BiblioFile Bibcat* (online public access catalog), *BiblioFile Serials Control*, *BiblioFile Cataloging*, and *BiblioFile Acquisitions*.

Serials

Tracking a serials collection manually is time consuming, to say the least. With a computer, many of the tasks are easily automated. One very bothersome chore associated with serials is routing them to different faculty or executives in a corporation. The programs below will not only keep track of the process, but even print the routing slips.

I was not fully aware of the many problems inherent in routing periodicals to various people within a corporation when the first edition of this book was published. Since then, several people have asked me if any software could assist in this task. There are several listed below, I am happy to say.

Name:	**Card Datalog Serials Software**
Program type:	Serials management
Vendor:	Data Trek
Cost:	Contact Data Trek. Sample disk available free.
Hardware requirements:	IBM and compatibles, Macintosh, DEC/VAX
Description:	Program offers wide range of serials management. As serials are received, they may be checked in with just a single keystroke, once the library has entered basic information about the periodical. Program will also project volume issue and date. Routing slips can be generated automatically, including multiple issues. Other features include patron access through printed holdings lists by title or subject, and online searching access.

Name:	**Checkmate II**
Program type:	Serials control system
Vendor:	CLASS
Cost:	$3,300, nonCLASS member; $2,970, CLASS member
Hardware requirements:	IBM and compatibles
Description:	Excellent system will control a serials collection and has been in existence for many years. It was developed by

CLASS, a library network. Will perform check-in, claims, and routing. Check-in is with cursor control. Creates sorted lists for monthly reports. Allows for keyword searching, Boolean logic, and truncated searching. Records and fields may be user-defined. Up to 30,000 records may be handled by the system.

Documentation: Binder of start-up information and instructions. Records may also be downloaded from EBSCO by EBSCO subscription customers.

Name: **Corporate Document Control**
Program type: Document retrieval
Vendor: Right On Programs
Cost: $299
Hardware requirements: IBM and compatibles, with hard-disk drive recommended
Description: This easy-to-operate program comes ready to run. It is primarily useful to a library that acquires a large number of documents, such as annual reports, quarterly reports, and proxies. They can be easily entered into the system and then searched for by company name, company identification number, or acronym. The main menu provides for adding a company, edit or display a company, and search for overdue reports. When an overdue is noted, a request letter can be generated by the system. It can limit how long documents are to be retained. Purge dates will cull dated material to free up space. Extremely simple to use. Particularly useful for corporate libraries.
Documentation: Booklet

Name: **Periodical Manager**
Program type: Internal magazine and journal circulation
Vendor: Right On Programs
Cost: $229
Hardware requirements: IBM and compatibles
Description: Contains all features of *Subscription Manager* and *Routing Manager*, both discussed below. Will track periodicals as they are circulated internally in a corporation or other business. Will also track periodical subscriptions, including those received and not received. Tracks title, orders, number, etc. Lists for one or all can be printed. Address labels can be printed. Keeps a record of payments, accounts receivable, and statement information.
Documentation: Simple booklet

Name:	**Remo: Automated Serials Management System**
Program type:	Serials management
Vendor:	Readmore
Cost:	$19.95; inquire about other options available
Hardware requirements:	IBM and compatibles
Description:	System is a sophisticated package for tracking serials. Features include creating bibliographies, Boolean logic searching, and an interface for MARC records. System will check serials in, claim, mark for bindery, create statistical reports, and generate purchase orders. Networking is also an option. System contains its own database management system for creating reports. Menu-driven, but this function can be uncoupled.
Review sources:	*Serials Review*, vol. 14, no. 4, 1988, 21.

Name:	**Routing Manager**
Program type:	Magazine and periodical routing
Vendor:	Right On Programs
Cost:	$129
Hardware requirements:	IBM and compatibles
Description:	Database program lists all magazines and people to whom they are routed. A new person is typed into the database whenever necessary. Persons in the database may be given a priority number from 0 to 9, where 9 is the lowest priority, and 0 the highest. Multiple copies may be routed in several ways: alphabetically, by priority number, or both. Additional nonrouted copies may be sent wherever needed. A search may also be made by magazine title to determine who is receiving it, or by person to see which magazines each is receiving. Routing slips will accommodate a top and bottom message, library heading, and date. Routing slips are printed as needed. Special routing paper, perforated horizontally, four to a page, can be ordered from Right On Programs.
Documentation:	Simple booklet

Name:	**Serial Control**
Program type:	Periodical management
Vendor:	Right On Programs
Cost:	$169
Hardware requirements:	IBM and compatibles
Description:	This program provides an easy way to keep track of all magazines owned by the library. It is a readymade database for

serial control. Users type in the data about each issue, and a list of missing issues can be generated. In addition, the program provides a listing of periodicals soon to expire, which may be done by a first and last date. Routing is a main feature of this program. Periodicals may be designated as not routed. Changing or adding names is easy. About the only unfortunate aspect of the program is that it does not save data automatically unless the program is exited in a specified way. Otherwise, the file will be left open and its data will be garbled.

Documentation: Excellent step-by-step manual. Provides full installation instructions as well as guidance through the menus.

Name: **Subscription Manager**

Program type: Magazine and periodical acquisition

Vendor: Right On Programs

Cost: $129; can also be purchased with *Routing Manager* as package called *Periodical Manager*, $229

Hardware requirements: IBM and compatibles

Description: This program will well serve special libraries to keep track of subscriptions. Will track titles, orders placed, and number of subscriptions. A complete printout will quickly reveal which numbers are missing and which can be sent to supplier for claim. Also prints address labels for correspondence. Subscriptions may be batch processed once each year, or as necessary.

Related programs: *Routing Manager* and *Periodical Manager*.

Documentation: Simple booklet

Spreadsheets and Statistics

Spreadsheet and statistical software in general has undergone profound development over the past five years. The original electronic spreadsheet was VisiCalc. This electronic equivalent of the accountant's paper and pencil is no longer in production. It was simple yet sophisticated enough to meet the needs of nearly all libraries. Newer spreadsheets, however, will do more. For instance, some can take the data that the user has entered and perform not only statistical analysis but also create chart and graph representations, even in color.

Some products will then automatically incorporate the chart or graph into a printed report, often another module of the system, or allow the material to be cut and pasted into another package.

All spreadsheets have rows and columns of rectangles termed cells. Their size is one way to gauge a program's capability. Each cell may contain labels, raw data, or formulas for manipulating data. Once a spreadsheet has been created, it is termed a template and may be saved without the data for reuse at another time.

The most useful spreadsheet function in a library is at budget time. By entering the library's budget and using the correct formulas, a resulting spreadsheet will total the library's projected expenditures and income. If the two do not match, then a change (such as a reduction in the book budget) can be made, and the spreadsheet will automatically recalculate and report the new totals. This feature is exceptionally useful when working with a board of trustees.

Ease of use and a short learning curve may be more important to most libraries than sophistication, unless the spreadsheet is to be used every day. Even the simplest spreadsheets will prove useful to any library.

Name:	**ExpressCalc**
Program type:	Spreadsheet
Vendor:	Expressware Corporation
Cost:	$20

Hardware requirements:	IBM and compatibles
Description:	This is an easy way for most libraries to begin with the purchase and use of a powerful spreadsheet without investing very much money.

System will create spreadsheet of 64 columns by 256 lines, a decidedly smaller workspace than with most other leading competitors, but one that will be useful for most library budgeting functions.

Review sources:	*Library Software Review*, November–December 1987, 399.
Documentation:	A 190-page manual contains a modest tutorial and much reference material in dictionary format.

Name:	**Excel**
Program type:	Spreadsheet
Vendor:	Microsoft
Cost:	$395, Macintosh; $495, IBM
Hardware requirements:	Macintosh; IBM and compatibles.
Description:	*Excel* is a powerful spreadsheet that comes with a version of *Windows* for the IBM version. The two packages interface together very well, allowing the power of the spreadsheet to be easily used and learned with the user-friendly *Windows* operating system.

Either version, the IBM or the Macintosh, is quite good. The Mac version will use any font installed in the Mac system. A special preview option allows for a page preview prior to printing.

The program has 21 built-in formats. Users can create more using macros. It will also produce 44 types of charts, including area, bar, column, pie, line, and scatter. It will not produce three-dimensional charts.

System will interact well with certain programs, namely Microsoft *Word*, a word processing package. An *Excel* spreadsheet used within a *Word* document allows for changing the spreadsheet and automatically changing the word processing document, which can save a lot of time. *Excel* is also programmed with drivers for various printers, including HP laser printers and Apple LaserWriter II.

Review sources:	*Library Software Review*, September–October, 1988, 361.
Documentation:	The manual is massive and excellent at over 700 pages. Also comes with installation guide and quick reference guide.

Name:	**Quattro Pro**
Program type:	Spreadsheet

Vendor:	Borland International, Inc.
Cost:	$495
Hardware requirements:	IBM and compatibles, with hard-disk drive
Description:	*Quattro Pro* is considered an excellent advanced spreadsheet, offering as many features as any of the newer and more powerful packages on the market today. In the context of an advanced business package, it may prove an unnecessarily powerful purchase for most library needs.

The program allows for larger spreadsheets because its ·dynamic memory is reallocated on a hard-disk drive, making excessive RAM space not necessary. Spreadsheet capacity is 256 columns by 8192 rows.

The system is more powerful than many others available since it will allow up to 32 spreadsheets to be active or open simultaneously in separate windows. Through the window function, each spreadsheet may be moved, resized, or activated on screen as needed.

As many as 63 spreadsheets may be linked together, creating spreadsheet interaction on a vast scale.

Graphics for this program are very good, including the ability to create bar, line, stacked, and pie charts.

Review sources:	*Library Software Review*, November–December, 1988, 430.
Documentation:	Excellent manual that provides illustrations and material

Training Programs for Computer Skills

Training programs can be useful for both staff and public. Videotape training programs can be circulated as part of the regular video collection. Specific training programs for specific software are also available.

Some programs provide tutorials on disk with the original package. Examples are those of *AppleWorks* and *WordPerfect*.

Name:	**BRS/After Dark CAI Simulation**
Program type:	Online practice tutorial
Vendor:	MecklerSoft
Cost:	$69.95
Hardware requirements:	Apple II series
Description:	The point of this program is to give the user experience with an online service without having to pay online fees for training. The process of exploring BRS becomes quite manageable as it is broken into small parts, each one a lesson. Some of the BRS features that will be learned include creating and executing an online search strategy. Instruction is totally self-paced. The program is menu-driven.
Review sources:	*Library Software Review*, November–December, 1988, 433.
Documentation:	Manual of instructions, which includes search worksheets

Name:	**Call Number Order (Dewey and Fiction)**
Program type:	Library skills
Vendor:	CALICO
Cost:	$24.95
Hardware requirements:	Apple II series
Description:	This program is a tutorial for teaching new employees how to use the Dewey system. It can also be used for students or general public and will handle both review and testing.
Documentation:	Simple booklet, but all that is needed

Name: **Library of Congress Call Number Order**
Program type: Library skills
Vendor: CALICO
Cost: $29.95
Hardware requirements: Apple II series
Description: Same concept as the program above, this one concentrates on teaching, reviewing and testing for the Library of Congress Classification system. Good for both employees, students, and general patrons. For grade 10 through adult.
Documentation: Simple booklet, but all that is needed.

Name: **Macintosh and IBM Video Training**
Program type: Videotape instruction learning system
Vendor: MacProfessional Learning Systems, Inc.
Cost: $59.95 per tape
Hardware requirements: Videocassette player
Description: Excellent tapes and selection of computer programs for the Macintosh and IBM computers. Subjects cover many software packages, DOS, and more. Included are: *Hyper-Card Basics, Word, Excel, PageMaker, Adobe Illustrator, WordPerfect, dBase, WordStar Professional, Children and Computers*, and many more.
Documentation: Self-documenting

Name: **Using Dissertation Abstracts International**
Program type: Online practice tutorial
Vendor: MecklerSoft
Cost: $59.95
Hardware requirements: Apple II series
Description: Capable program introduces students or employees to *Dissertation Abstracts International* and *Comprehensive Dissertation Index*. It teaches at or around the graduate level. Seven sections explain DAI. Students start with pretest and go on to lessons as they wish. It is easy to use.
Review sources: *Library Software Review*, November–December, 1988, 433.
Documentation: Notebook sufficiently explains system.

Name: **Video Professor Series**
Program type: IBM and Macintosh video training
Vendor: Special Interest Videos
Cost: $29.95 per tape (package deals available)
Hardware requirements: Videocassette player

Description: This excellent series of videotapes teaches basic skills for DOS and a variety of important programs.

IBM topics include *Lotus 1-2-3, WordPerfect, WordStar, Word, dBase 3 and 4, PFS: First Choice* (spreadsheet and word processor), *PFS: First Publisher, Works* (word processing), *Ventura, Windows, MultiMate Advantage II* (word processing), and *Excel.*

Macintosh tapes include *Word, MacWrite, Excel, Wing Z, PageMaker, WordPerfect, Quark XPress, Freehand, Adobe Illustrator, Deneba Canvas,* and *Silicon Beach Superpaint.* Also available are *AppleWorks* (database, spreadsheet, and word processing), and tapes for kids and computer hardware. For both beginners and advanced users.

Documentation: Self-documenting

Utilities

An infinite number of software utilities is available for microcomputers. These fall into the categories of software enhancements, virus protection, backup protection, and file and disk organization.

Virus protection and eradication programs are becoming more popular and more effective. One is a good investment, especially for computers with more than one user, or if other computers' files are downloaded. Downloading is a primary way of receiving a virus.

Backing up programs or duplicating an entire file, especially from a hard-disk drive, is vital. To back up an entire hard-disk drive can be tricky and time-consuming. Some programs will do it automatically—all the user has to do is to change disks as requested.

Files and disk organization programs are very useful. Packages such as *TreeTop* will make it easy to work with many files. Such programs will alphabetize, search, block delete, copy, and do most DOS functions more efficiently.

The original utilities made copies of individual programs that were otherwise uncopyable. Manufacturers often do not want people to copy their programs, so they make them difficult to copy. With the use of special utility programs that contain copy parameters, most programs can be backed up.

Name:	**Copy II +**
Program type:	Backup copy program
Vendor:	Central Point Software
Cost:	$40
Hardware requirements:	Apple II series; Macintosh
Description:	This program has been around for many years and continues to be popular. It can be used in two different ways. The first is as a straightforward copy program. If it does not work, then some alteration of the parameters can be made and the program will try again. Another way is to use the built-in parameters for many programs. Many are for popular arcade games.

Documentation:	Excellent manual describing procedures for making backups, how to get the most of the program, and other useful information

Name:	**LifeSaver**
Program type:	Data reconstruction
Vendor:	Follett Software
Cost:	$35
Hardware requirements:	Apple II series
Description:	When a data disk has crashed, this program can be used to retrieve any useful data left. Program meticulously analyzes disk and writes salvageable data to new disk. Also checks drive timing for problems. Can be used on Apple II DOS 3.3, ProDOS, Pascal, and CP/M files.
Documentation:	Simple booklet giving instructions

Name:	**The Norton Utilities, Advanced Edition**
Program type:	Disk utilities
Vendor:	Peter Norton Computing, Inc.
Cost:	$150
Hardware requirements:	IBM and compatibles
Description:	Popular and highly useful set of utilities for IBM and compatibles, providing a major enhancement of DOS features. Twenty-four separate programs in this package will assist in lost data recovery, the repair of hard-disk drives, manage data, and speed up the disk drive. The program comes with its own integrator or file management–menu system, or programs can be used directly from DOS.
	The beep utility will play tones through speakers. The disk test utility checks disk and files for physical damage. The file find utility will search for a file or directory that cannot otherwise be found on a disk or disks. The file info utility will add descriptive annotations to file and directory names. The main program utility is a set of three programs that will create a map of disk usage, including space available. It also has an unerase feature for recovering lost files.
	This package is exceptionally easy to learn to use and very useful for most people. Worth the investment.
Review sources:	*Library Software Review*, September–October, 1988, 359.
Documentation:	Excellent manual, which describes how to use each program

Name:	**TreeTop**
Program type:	Hard-disk file and directory manager

Vendor:	Kilgore Software
Cost:	$39 (shareware product)
Hardware requirements:	IBM and compatibles
Description:	When a hard-disk drive, especially a very large one, has been in service for a while, it may contain large numbers of files and programs. This utility package is a quick and easy way to organize beyond the usual root and subdirectories that are available with MS and PC-DOS. Files may be sorted by name, extension, size, date and time, ascending or descending order. They may be copied, moved, deleted, or printed as single files or groups. Some of the features not found on all of the other major directory programs available include tagging files by date and time range, pull-down menus, mouse support, and indicating directories with tagged files on directory tree.
Documentation:	A printed bound manual gives instructions and uses

Vertical File

Special collections of materials, such as pamphlets and booklets, brochures, and ephemera can be difficult to locate and track. Any file management system will make an inventory list of materials. The ready-made program by Right On Programs below negates the need to set up a database structure from scratch. *Vertical File on Diskette* is a set of vertical file articles grouped by different subjects. They can be searched and are never in danger of being lost or misplaced in the wrong folder unless the disk's contents are lost. Refiling materials is not necessary when students are finished with some aspects of computer database searching.

Name:	**Vertical File Resource Material on Micro-Computer Diskette**
Program type:	Online vertical file
Vendor:	Educational Resource and Research Service
Cost:	$25 to $63 per subject disk; subscription available
Hardware requirements:	Apple II series
Description:	This program automates the use of the vertical file by patrons. It dispenses with storage of paper copies, making electronic access quick and reliable. There are approximately 25 full-text articles per disk. The disk on drugs, for example, contains various viewpoints on that subject. Making a printout is a simple one-key operation. Material is always in the computer, and refiling, unlike paper copies, is not necessary. A partial list of available titles includes abortion, aging, alcoholism, arms control, child abuse, crime, cults, diseases, drugs, gun control, hunger, minorities, pollution, prisons, terrorism, and water.
Documentation:	A single page of instructions is all that patrons will need.
Name:	**Vertical File Locator**
Program type:	Vertical file database
Vendor:	Right On Programs

Cost: $89

Hardware requirements: IBM and compatibles; Apple II series

Description: This simple system organizes vertical file material. Each pamphlet or item is given an accession number and up to two subject headings, eliminating the need for traditional filing in alphabetical order. Simple numerical (accession) order will suffice. As materials are returned to the library after circulation, they may be put quickly back into numerical order. The printed subject list allows for quick retrieval of material in two places instead of the traditional single location of an alphabetical vertical file listing.

Related programs: Many database programs will do this type of operation. See the section on databases in this volume. Most require some additional set-up time and learning.

Documentation: Simple and easy to follow

Videotape Control

There were no packages for videotape control in the first edition of this book. Since then, however, videotapes have become big business in libraries. Some libraries circulate thousands of tapes each month, making their careful control crucial. The two systems below are simple reservation and circulation systems with one special facet: they handle only videotapes.

Sometimes it is not possible for a library with an online system to include videotapes in the system for technical or other reasons (there may be no money for an additional terminal near the tapes). Libraries that do not have an online system for books may find that an online system for videotapes is both economical and worthwhile, since it can be used with a minimum of effort.

Both of the systems below can handle libraries with these particular needs.

Name:	**On-Line Video Catalog**
Program type:	Online catalog
Vendor:	Right On Programs
Cost:	$199
Hardware requirements:	IBM and compatibles
Description:	A very simple-to-use program allows users to create an on-line catalog of videotape holdings. Videotapes may be searched by keyword (up to six), title, or director. A list of videos then appears on the screen, giving brief information about those that satisfy the search criteria. Additional information about each appears in an onscreen catalog card. Staff may print a holdings list whenever desired. Password protected.
Documentation:	Booklet

Name:	**Video Reserve Control**
Program type:	Videotape reservation system
Vendor:	Right On Programs
Cost:	$99

Hardware requirements: IBM and compatibles

Description: For libraries with small videotape collections, this program can solve the problem of circulating tapes to patrons, teachers, or students. Data is entered at screen prompts: title, rating, running time, patron reserve information (name, address, telephone, etc.). Database may then be recalled by title, rating or subject. Report of video circulation is available to help track collection development needs. User friendly.

Documentation: Simple booklet of instructions

Word Processing and Accessories

Word processors are the easiest type of software to master. More people probably use a word processing program successfully than any other type of software, with good reason. The word processor is the computer's version of the typewriter, with which we are already familiar.

The microcomputer as word processor is far more than a glorified typewriter. The more sophisticated the package, the more function keys and other complications that will exist. With a typical program, the user inputs data for a letter or report using the keyboard. The input material can then be saved to disk and stored for any amount of time, loaded back into the computer, revised and altered, and printed. It may then be saved and stored again. The most important aspect of word processing is the editing capability it offers. Wholesale changes may be made to a document without retyping it. The computer does all of the retyping.

In addition to typing and cut-and-paste tasks, most word processors with spell checkers can search for incorrectly spelled words. Used in conjunction with other programs, the word processor can also check the document for grammar errors and other problems. It will not find everything, but it will correct many typographical errors.

Documents can be printed out as hardcopy or saved to disk. Printed documents can be mailed to a distant location while the electronic version can be sent by modem over the phone lines.

Some word processors, such as that component in *AppleWorks*, are very simple products, unable to produce documents with columns or graphics. Others, such as *WordPerfect*, are able to do just about anything. *AppleWorks* is excellent for most small and medium-sized libraries. If the library's needs ever expand, however, it may have to switch word processors. A program such as *WordPerfect* will grow with the library, since it has highly sophisticated features. Learning *WordPerfect* is correspondingly difficult.

Even with the best word processing program and computer, the final copy will only be as good as the output device. A poor-quality printer or a poor ribbon will make a poor finished product.

Can we throw away the typewriter? We still need it to type small cards, labels, and notes, and we need it as the ultimate backup when the computer goes down and an essential letter must still get out. Keep the typewriter and computer side by side.

In addition to the products below, some very capable word processors are described in the integrated software section of this book.

Name:	**Classroom News International**
Program type:	Student word processing/public access
Vendor:	Educational Activities, Inc.
Cost:	$295
Hardware requirements:	Apple II series
Description:	This program is particularly good for teaching young people from grade 5 and up the benefits of word processing. Although it can be useful, it lacks the power of more sophisticated word processors. Students can quickly use it to create classroom or school newsletters (including two columns), to work in Spanish, German, and French, and more. For an educational word processing system, it has a surprising amount of power. It can use ASCII files created with other systems or downloaded from a modem, print in color, and use multiple workspaces.
Documentation:	Manual contains instructions plus a set of reproducible activity masters for classroom use.

Name:	**Grammatik III**
Program type:	Grammar and punctuation checker
Vendor:	Reference Software Inc.
Cost:	$99
Hardware requirements:	IBM and compatibles, with hard-disk drive
Description:	A simple program for evaluating grammar and punctuation in text documents, it will check for errors and suspect grammar and then ask user to make the final decisions. The program cannot be used as a grammar crutch, since it won't find everything—not every "catch" might be wrong, or the user's own use of grammar might be better. It is easy to use and can be customized for individual use. Typical errors and writing problems found by the program are homonyms, possessives, transpositions, disagreement of subject and verb, redundant comparatives, incomplete sentences, double negatives, and split infinitives.
Review sources:	*Electronic Learning*, March 1989, 55.
	Classroom Computer Learning, May–June 1989, 15.

Documentation:	All necessary information is contained in excellent, extensive documentation. List of error messages, directions on how to customize program with selected phrases, and step-by-step walkthrough instructions are included.

Name:	**PC-Write**
Program type:	Word processor
Vendor:	Quicksoft Inc.
Cost:	$89 (shareware)
Hardware requirements:	IBM and compatibles
Description:	This word processor is an exceptionally good value, especially since it can be obtained and used for a trial period without any obligation. It will perform many advanced feats and is the most that many users will ever need. Some complications are often noted, including the spelling program not being as easy to use as those in many other word processors. Also, customizing the program for special uses can be extremely difficult. Other products to expand the system with graphics and other add-ons are available through the same publisher.
Review sources:	*Byte*, March 1989, 98.
	PC Magazine, January 31, 1989, 38.
Documentation:	Comes with instruction manual. Program can be given away freely to anyone, but can be used after a trial period only if registration fee is sent to publisher.

Name:	**RightWriter**
Program type:	Grammar and style checker
Vendor:	RightSoft
Cost:	$95
Hardware requirements:	IBM and compatibles
Description:	This program is one of the better grammar and style checkers available. Upon checking a document, it provides a myriad of suggestions for improvement. The suggestions are embedded in the text. Spelling is taken into account, as are two identical words in a row, grammar, etc. A printout can be produced upon completion. I found *RightWriter* an excellent aid. My only complaint was the amount of time that was required to go back through a document and reword it according to the suggestions. Few people could afford the time to run every document through it, so selected or occasional documents might be a compromise. Also, the better your

writing becomes, the less time it takes to check it with *RightWriter*.

Review sources:	*InfoWorld*, September 1988, 52.
	Computer Shopper, October 1989, 372.
Documentation:	Easy-to-read manual details most of the style problems highlighted in the program with suggestions for overcoming them.

Name:	**Sensible Grammar**
Program type:	Grammar and style checker
Vendor:	Sensible Software
Cost:	$99.95
Hardware requirements:	Apple II series; Macintosh
Description:	Splendid package corrects many simple but often overlooked grammatical errors. Not a word processor or spelling program, *Sensible Grammar* is intended for use with files created by other programs, most particularly word processing packages. Setup is simple: it is preprogrammed for a number of word processors. Just select a procedure from setup menu. An offending or "suspect" phrase is highlighted on screen. User selects appropriate choice such as mark, enter, print it, replace it, or ignore it. Considerable flexibility is allowed in the selection of the database that the program uses to check files. Categories include cliches, contractions, legal terms, and faulty, informal, personal, redundant, vague, or wordy phrases. The program is very much like a tutor, since users learn as they work, making their subsequent documents more acceptable as errors are avoided. Also, there is no embarrassment, as when one person edits another's work.
Review sources:	*MacWorld*, August 1988, 145.
	Macuser, December 1988, 67.
Documentation:	Excellent notebook contains extensive setup instructions. Manual can be used as a good reference book, describing operation, error handling, utilities, and much more in easy-to-follow format. Indexed.

Name:	**Sensible Speller**
Program type:	Word processor accessory
Vendor:	Sensible Software
Cost:	$125
Hardware requirements:	Apple II series

Description:	Getting started with this program takes a few seconds or up to 20 minutes, depending on customization. Unlike earlier spell checkers that required that errors be marked with user-selected symbols and corrected later with word processing program, this fully capable spelling program can be used with documents and word processors that did not come with a built-in spelling correction module.
Related programs:	Works with most Apple II word processing packages, including *WordStar*.
Documentation:	Easy to use and flexible, with ability to increase dictionary size, change drives or slot numbers, utilize upper- and lowercase, etc.

Name:	**Word**
Program type:	Word processor
Vendor:	Microsoft
Cost:	$450
Hardware requirements:	Macintosh; IBM and compatibles
Description:	This is perhaps the best word processor for the Macintosh. It does not have nearly the power of *WordPerfect*, though it is far easier to use. Getting started takes only minutes, and work can be performed without much effort. It makes good use of the window environment and mouse. The spell checker module makes it possible to check a document without touching the keyboard.
Documentation:	Excellent large binder

Name:	**Word Finder**
Program type:	Electronic thesaurus
Vendor:	Microlytics, Inc.
Cost:	$79.95, IBM; $59.95, Macintosh
Hardware requirements:	Apple II series; IBM and compatibles; Macintosh
Description:	An add-on product, *Word Finder* is the electronic version of the old-fashioned print thesaurus. It has 15,000 key words and 220,000 synonyms. Most librarians are familiar with spelling programs but not with this particular type of writing aid. An important question is, "Is this an improvement over the printed thesaurus widely in use?" Although I have personally decided to keep my hard copy for the foreseeable future, I did find at least one advantage to this version: speed. With the electronic version, users do not turn through pages of text, looking for a synonym; words appear on the screen from within the word processor. For thoroughness,

the printed book offers an in-depth analysis of relationships between words, categories, and parts of speech (noun, adjective, etc.), but the computerized version excels in quick changes, operated from the keyboard.

Word Finder can be up and running in about five minutes and may be operated from within or outside a word-processing program. After it is loaded, it can be summoned by a two-key stroke sequence. The cursor highlights the word in question. A list of synonyms is displayed on the bottom half of the screen and the user quickly and easily substitutes any word—or none—with a keystroke.

The program may also be used without a word processor, though the word-replacement feature does not work perfectly. It may be reconfigured to a different word processor. *Word Finder* can be used with several different word processing programs for the IBM as well as in a generic mode.

Review sources: *MacWeek*, November 10, 1987, 30.
MacWorld, February 1988, 206.

Documentation: Short booklet explains system adequately.

Name: **WordPerfect**
Program type: Word processor
Vendor: Word Perfect Corporation
Cost: $495
Hardware requirements: IBM and compatibles; Apple IIGS; Macintosh
Description: This word processor has recently surpassed all others in popularity. It is extremely sophisticated. Its only real problem is the time required to understand and memorize all of the forty plus function keys. The excellent and easily accessible online help file as well as a plastic keypad overlay will help the beginner.

WordPerfect is the fifth word processor I have used since becoming involved with microcomputers. In my opinion, it far surpasses *WordStar*, *AppleWorks*, or even Microsoft *Word*. Every feature is available, though sometimes it may be hard to find something. The program is, however, worth the investment in time. It will expand whenever your needs change or you need to go the extra mile.

Features include column format, math functions, sort routines, macros, graphics, and much more.

The spell checker is quite excellent. It operates with one keystroke and is very efficient. Users may add words to the dictionary as they go along. Additional sessions to correct spelling should be correspondingly shorter as a result.

WordPerfect for the Macintosh includes WYSIWYG (what you see is what you get) screen format. The user can change fonts and see the results on the screen. Two pages can be reduced in size for previewing on the screen, side by side.

Review sources: *ITC Desktop*, March–April 1989, 64.
Macuser, February 1989, 212.

Related programs: *WordPerfect Library*; *WordPerfect Office*

Documentation: Outstanding manual encompasses tutorial, reference, and glossary.

Name: **WordStar Professional**

Program type: Word processor

Vendor: MicroPro International Corporation

Cost: $495; $595, for LAN version

Hardware requirements: IBM and compatibles

Description: This is the original "what you see is what you get" word processor, and it has been very popular from the beginning of the microcomputer revolution. Text is formatted on the screen during composition exactly as it is to be printed out. Longtime users will find that the product has been regularly improved and is now much easier to use. It uses function and control key combinations for editing and allows three different types of help screens or none at all.

This new professional version includes desktop publishing features to enhance its usefulness. A subprogram called Inset will print graphics and text on the same page, will search files, and will handle telecommunications. Star Exchange allows the conversion of files from other word processors for use with *WordStar*.

A separate LAN version is available.

Review sources: *Personal Computing*, August 1989, 719.
PC Today, December 1989, 21.

Documentation: Excellent manual contains illustrations, examples, and instructions.

Computer Periodicals of Interest

A+, Box 52324, Boulder, CO 80321

Apple Library Users Group Newsletter, 10381 Bandley Drive M/S 8C, Cupertino, CA 95014

Byte, Subscription Dept., Box 6807, Piscataway, NJ 08855

CD-ROM Librarian, Meckler Publishing Corporation, 11 Ferry Lane West, Westport, CT 06880

Computers and the Media Center, 515 Oak Street North, Cannon Falls, MN 55009

Computers in Libraries (formerly *Small Computers in Libraries*), Meckler Publishing Corporation, 11 Ferry Lane West, Westport, CT 06880

Connect: Libraries and Telecommunications, Steve Cisler, 625 Barnacle Way, Suisun, CA 94585

The Electronic Library, Learned Information, 143 Old Marlton Pike, Medford, NJ 08055

Family and Home Office Computing, Scholastic, Inc., 730 Broadway, NY, NY 10003

Information Technology and Libraries, American Library Association, 50 East Huron Street, Chicago, IL 60611

InfoWorld, Box 1018, Southeastern, PA 19398

Library Hi Tech, Pierian Press, Box 1808, Ann Arbor, MI 48016

Library Hi Tech News, Pierian Press, Box 1808, Ann Arbor, MI 48016

Library Software Review, Meckler Publishing Corporation, 11 Ferry Lane West, Westport, CT 06880

MacWorld, Subscription Dept., Box 51666, Boulder, CO 80321

Technicalities, M. E. Sharpe, Inc., 80 Business Park Drive, Armonk, NY 11504

Company Addresses and Product Information

Addison Public Library

235 North Kennedy Drive

Addison, IL 60101

Phone for orders or product information: (708) 543-3617. Products include: catalog card and label production.

Aldus Corporation

411 First Avenue, South, Suite 200

Seattle, WA 98104

(206) 622-5500.

Ashton-Tate

20101 Hamilton Avenue

Torrance, CA 90502

Orders and product information:

(213) 329-8000.

Banner Blue

Box 7865

Fremont, CA 94537

Orders and product information:

(415) 794-6850.

Bar Scan, Inc.

Box 19091

Irvine, CA 92713

(714) 259-9797

Brodart Co.

500 Arch Street

Williamsport, PA 17701

Orders and product information: (717) 326-2461 (ext. 640). Company founded: 1939. Software cannot be ordered over phone. Salesperson will consult with library upon request.

Broderbund

17 Paul Drive

San Rafael, CA 94903.

BRS Software Products

Division of Maxwell Online Services

8000 Westpark Drive

McLean, VA 22102

Product information: (703) 442-3870; Orders: (800) 235-1209. Company founded: 1976. Products include: full, free text software thesaurus, data entry.

ButtonWare, Inc.

Box 5786

Bellevue, WA 98006

Orders and product information:

(800) 528-8866; (206) 454-0479.

C P International Inc.

210 South Street

New York, NY 10002

(212) 815-8691

CALICO (Computer Assisted Library Information Co.), Inc.

Box 15916
St. Louis, MO 63114
Orders and product information: (800) 367-0416. Company founded: 1981. Products include: reference tutorials for library skills, integrated library system. Company founded by librarians.

Capital PC–Users Group

51 Monroe Street, Plaza East Two
Rockville, MD 20850
Orders or product information: (301) 762-6557. Has large catalog of shareware products for low prices.

Caspr

10311 South DeAnza Boulevard
Cupertino, CA 95014
Phone for orders or product information: (800) 852-2777. Company founded: 1985. Products include: integrated library system software, online public access catalog, catalog card and label production software.

Center for the Study of Rural Librarianship

College of Library Science
Clarion University
Clarion, PA 16214
Orders and product information: (814) 226-2271. Company founded: 1978. Only product is *OutputM*. Satisfaction guaranteed; product may be returned for full refund if not satisfied.

Charles W. Clark Co, Inc.

170 Keyland Court
Bohemia, NY 11716
Orders and product information: (800) 247-7009. Company founded: 1904. Products include: library management software.

Claris Corporation

Box 526
Santa Clara, CA 95052
Orders and product information:
(800) 544-8554.

CLASS

1415 Koll Circle, Suite 101
San Jose, CA 95112
Orders and product information:
(408) 453-0444. Founded: 1976.

Cognetics Corporation

55 Princeton-Highstown Road
Princeton Junction, NJ 08550
(609) 799-5005.

Columbia Computing Services

8101 East Prentice Avenue, Suite 700
Englewood, CO 80111
(800) 663-0544.

Data Trek, Inc.

167 Saxony Road
Encinitas, CA 92024
Orders and product information:
(800) 876-5484; (619) 436-5055.

Datastorm Technologies

Box 1471
Columbia, MO 65205
(314) 449-7012.

DCA/Crosstalk Communications

1000 Holcomb Woods Parkway
Roswell, GA 30076
(404) 998-3998.

Diakon Systems

3801 Glenmont Drive
Fort Worth, TX 76133.

Educational Activities, Inc.

Box 392
Freeport, NY 11520

Orders and product information: (800) 645-3739 (US); (516) 223-4666 (NY); FAX: (516) 623-9282. Products include: educational. Thirty-day preview of products available to educators. Toll-free hot line for technical support.

Educational Resource & Research Service (ER&RS)
Box 66
Barnesville, MN 56514
Orders or product information: (800) 752-4243; (218) 493-4587; (218) 354-7666.

Electronic Bookshelf
R.R. 9, Box 64
Frankfort, IN 46401.

Embar Information Consultants, Inc.
1234 Folkstone Drive
Wheaton, IL 60187
Orders and product information: (708) 668-1742. Company founded: 1984.

Follett Software Company
4506 Northwest Highway
Crystal Lake, IL 60014
Orders and product information: (815) 455-4660 (IL); (800) 323-3397.

The Foundation for Library Research, Inc.
2764 U.S. 35 South
Southside, WV 25187
Orders and product information:
(304) 675-4350.

FreeSoft Company
150 Hickory Drive
Beaver Falls, PA 15010
(412) 846-2700.

Galacticomm, Inc.
4101 Southwest 47th Avenue, Suite 101
Ft. Lauderdale, FL 33314
Orders and product information: (305) 583-5990; (305) 583-7808 (BBS).

Gaylord Information Systems
Box 4901
Syracuse, NY 13221
Orders and product information: (315) 457-5070.

General Research Corporation
5383 Hollister Avenue
Santa Barbara, CA 93111.

G-N-G Software
919 West Canadian Street
Vinita, OK 74301
Orders and product information: (918) 256-8598. Company founded: 1981. Software includes: library administration. Brochure available.

Hayes Microcomputer Products
507 Westech Drive
Norcross, GA 30092
(404) 441-1617.

Highlighted Data
4350 North Fairfax Drive, Suite 450
Arlington, VA 22203.

Hilgrave, Inc.
Box 941
Monroe, MI 48161
(313) 243-0576 or (800) 826-2760.

Information Access Company
362 Lakeside Drive
Foster City, CA 94404
Orders and product information:
(800) 227-8431.

Information Resources Publications
030 Huntington Hall, Syracuse University
Syracuse, NY 13244
Orders and product information: (315) 443-3640. Company founded: 1982. Products include: online search simulator.

Information Transform, Inc.
502 Leonard Street
Madison, WI 53711
Orders and product information: (608) 255-4800. Company founded: 1977. Products include: retrospective conversion, MARC record creation on PCs and Apple IIs.

InMagic, Inc.
2067 Massachusetts
Cambridge, MA 02140
(617) 661-8124.

IRIS Software Products
Box 57
Stoughton, MA 02072
(617) 341-1969.

IVY Systems Limited
E-5, Qutab Hotel
New Delhi, India 100 061
Orders and product information: 686 3901
(Pratap Raju or V.K. Gupta). Company
founded: 1989. Products include: multilingual DTP and information management
systems.

Kilgore Software
Box 2291
West Sacramento, CA 95691
Orders and product information:
(916) 371-3715.

Knowledge Access International
2685 Marine Way, Suite 1305
Mountain View, CA 94043
Orders and product information:
(415) 969-0606.

Leading Edge Software Products, Inc.
21 Highland Circle
Needham Heights, MA 02194
Orders and product information:
(800) 343-3436; (617) 449-4655.

Lee Library
Interlibrary Loan Department
Brigham Young University
Provo, UT 84602
(801) 378-6344

LEI, Inc.
R.R. 1, Box 219
New Albany, PA 18833
(717) 746-1842.

Library Automation Products
352 7th Avenue, Suite 1001
New York, NY 10001
Orders and product information: (212) 967-5418. Company founded: 1986. Products include: library automation software, *The Assistant*.

The Library Corporation
Box 40035
Washington, DC 20016
(800) 624-0559.

Library Processes System
919 West Canadian Street
Vinita, OK 74301
Orders and product information: (918) 256-8598. Company founded: 1981.

Looking Glass Learning Products, Inc.
276 East Howard Street
Des Plaines, IL 60018
Orders and product information: (800) 545-5457. Company founded: 1987. Products include: K–12 instruction.

Lutke, Robert E.
432 Cottage Avenue
Vermillion, SD 57069
Orders and product information: (605) 624-2948. Company founded: 1983. Products include: bibliography preparation for term papers, theses, dissertations, class reading lists, etc.

MacProfessional Learning Systems
2090 South Nova Road, Suite 205 B
South Daytona, FL 32119
Orders and product information:
(904) 761-7576.

McCarthy-McCormach, Inc.
1440 Oak Hills Drive
Colorado Springs, CO 80919
Orders and product information: (800) 869-1446. Company founded: 1982. Products include: education software, teacher utilities. Company created by teachers for teachers.

Megahaus Corporation
5703 Oberlin Drive
San Diego, CA 92121
(619) 450-1230.

MecklerSoft
Meckler Publishing Corporation
11 Ferry Lane West
Westport, CT 06880
Orders and product information: (203) 226-6967. FAX: (203) 454-5840.

Micro-VTLS
1800 Kraft Drive
Blacksburg, VA 24060
Orders and product information: (703) 231-3605. Company founded: 1976. Products include: integrated library system.

Microlytics, Inc.
300 Main Street, Suite 516
East Rochester, NY 14445
(716) 377-0130 (NY); (800) 808-6293.

Microtech Consulting Co.
206 Angie Drive, Box 521
Cedar Falls, IA 50613
(800) 922-SIGN or (319) 277-6648.

Mousetrap Software
336 Coleman Drive
Monroeville, PA 15146
Orders and product information:
(412) 372-9004.

Mustang Software, Inc.
Box 2264
Bakersville, CA 93303
Orders and product information: (805) 395-0223; (805) 395-0650 (BBS).

OCLC, Inc.
6565 Frantz Road
Dublin, OH 43017
(614) 764-6000.

Oryx Press
4041 North Central Avenue
Phoenix, AZ 85004
Orders and product information:
(800) 457-6799.

Peachtree Software, Inc.
4355 International Boulevard
Norcross, GA 30093
Orders and product information:
(800) 247-3224; (800) 554-8900.

Persoft
465 Science Drive
Madison, WI 53711
Orders and product information:
(608) 273-6000.

Personal Bibliographic Software, Inc.
Box 4250
Ann Arbor, MI 48106
Orders and product information:
(313) 996-1580.

Peter Norton Computing, Inc.
2210 Wilshire Boulevard, #186
Santa Monica, CA 90403
Orders and product information:
(213) 453-2361.

Quarterdeck Office Systems
150 Pico Boulevard
Santa Monica, CA 90505
(213) 392-9701.

Rachels
Peter Konneker,
111 Innsbruck Drive
Clayton, NC 27520
Orders and product information: (919) 553-5511. Major products include several catalog card programs. Company founded: 1986.

Real Time Computer Services
1706 Bison Drive
Kalispell, MT 59901
Orders and product information: (406) 756-9079. Company founded: 1985.

Reference Software Inc.

330 Townsend Street, Suite 135
San Francisco, CA 94107
(800) 826-2222.

Right On Programs, Inc.

755 New York Avenue
Huntington, NY 11743
Orders and product information: (516) 424-7777. Products include a wide variety of library software for small and medium-sized libraries.

Richard K. Riley

Box 2227
Augusta, ME 04338
No phone. Company founded: 1981. Products include: catalog card production.

Ringgold Management Systems, Inc.

Box 368
Beaverton, OR 97075
(503) 645-3503.

Scarecrow Press

52 Liberty Street
Metuchen, NJ 08840
Orders and product information: (800) 537-7107. Library science book publisher.

Schedule Master Corporation

Box 920063
Norcross, GA 30092
Orders and product information:
(404) 662-0781.

ScholarChips Software, Inc.

2030 Powers Ferry Road, Suite 308
Atlanta, GA 30339
Orders and product information:
(404) 859-9418.

SEI

2360-J George Washington Highway
Yorktown, VA 23692
(804) 898-8386.

Sensible Software, Inc.

335 East Big Beaver, Suite 207
Troy, MI 48083
Orders and product information:
(313) 528-1950.

SilverPlatter Information, Inc.

37 Walnut Street
Wellesley Hills, MA 02181
Orders and product information: (617) 239-0306; FAX: (617) 235-1715.

Society for Visual Education, Inc.

1345 West Diversey Parkway
Chicago, IL 60614
Orders and product information:
(312) 525-1500.

Softsync/BLOC Publishing

Box 143376, 800 Douglas Entrance
Coral Gables, FL 33134
Orders and product information:
(800) 933-2537.

Special Interest Video

100 Enterprise Place, Box 7022
Dover, DE 19903
Orders and product information:
(800) 522-0502.

Springboard Software, Inc.

7808 Creekridge Circle
Minneapolis, MN 55435
Orders and product information:
(800) 654-6301, ext. 2000.

Sunburst Communications, Inc.

101 Castleton Street
Pleasantville, NY 10570
Orders and product information: (800) 628-8897. Company founded: 1982. Offers a wide variety of classroom instructional software. Thirty-day classroom trial. Lifetime warranty. Free upgrades. District purchase plans. Lab packs. Newsletter.

TimeWorks

444 Lake Cook Road
Deerfield, IL 60015
(708) 948-9200.

TPS Electronics

4047 Transport Street
Palo Alto, CA 94303
Orders and product information: (413) 856-6833. Company founded: 1978. Products include: barcode printing and reading.

Utlas International

80 Bloor Street West
Toronto, Ont., Canada M5S 2V1
(800) 387-2713.

Video Inc.

3450 Slade Run Drive
Falls Church, VA 22042
Orders and product information:
(800) 342-4336; (703) 241-2030;
FAX: (703) 536-9540.

Winnebago Software Co.

310 West Main Street, Box 430
Caledonia, MN 55921
Orders and product information: (800) 533-5430. Company founded: 1982. Offers complete retrospective conversion service, and software for total library automation.

Word Perfect Corporation

1555 North Technology Way
Orem, UT 84057
(801) 225-5000.

Writing Consultants

Techniplex, 300 Main Street
East Rochester, NY 14445
(800) 828-6293; (716) 377-0130.

Glossary

Acoustic coupler—A telecommunications device that converts digital computer signals to analog telephone signals using a telephone handset instead of direct connect wiring. More errorprone than direct connect.

Analog—The continuous wave signal used by the telephone line. A pattern is determined based on changes in the signal. Opposite of digital, which generates a series of separate (discrete) signals in the form of "1"s and "0"s.

ASCII—American Standard Code for Information Interchange is an agreed-upon standard of 128 letters and other symbols. Each symbol is represented by a set of seven digits (1s and 0s).

Assembler—A computer programming language that makes it possible for humans to interface with or create machine language programs.

Backup—A second or additional copy on a disk of a program or data.

BASIC—Beginner's All-Purpose Symbolic Instruction Code, originally created as a teaching language, which eventually gained a following as an important high-level computer language.

Batch—Multiple instructions or data executed as a group, often as if typed from the keyboard (especially when used as a macro).

Baud—Bits per second transmitted. Typically, data speed is 300 baud (300 bits per second), 1200, 2400, 9600, etc. Because each computer character requires about ten bits (including stop, start, etc., bits), these rates respectively amount to 30, 120, 240, etc., characters per second.

Bell-compatible—Both 103 Bell-compatible and 212A Bell-compatible refer to Bell Telephone standards. 103 refers to 300 baud and 212A refers to 1200 baud. Some modems are referred to as 103/212A or 300/1200 baud.

Binary—Numbering system that contains only "1"s and "0"s (on or off).

Bit—The smallest unit of information that a computer can process—either a "1" or a "0". Bits are combined into groups of eight or more to form a byte.

Boot—The process of starting up a computer to prepare it for service. Usually, a small "bootstrap" program is loaded in, automatically making it possible to load other programs. A cold boot is performed when the power to the unit is first turned on, a warm boot when the machine is already on but needs to be reset for some reason.

Buffer—A space in memory reserved for a special function, such as a storage place for material being printed, saved from screen, etc.

175

Bulletin board system—An interactive online database, which may have a number of features, including multiple lines in, upload/download of public domain and shareware programs, electronic mail, conference areas, etc. Usually, though not always, operated on a local microcomputer. Some operate on national networks such as the Source or CompuServe.

Bundled—Software that comes with hardware is "bundled" with the hardware. Often such a system includes a word processor and a database management system. The purpose of bundling is to make the product more marketable.

Byte—Generally, eight bits used during transmission, though stop and start bits may make it ten bits. A byte is basically a computer word (character) such as "W" or "1."

CAI—Computer-Assisted Instruction defines a lot of areas, but it is any program which attempts to teach a skill through computer drills or training.

CD-ROM—Compact Disk–Read Only Memory is a recently introduced storage device that differs in several important ways from conventional disk drives. It will hold several hundred megabytes of data and is more difficult to damage or erase. A major problem with CD-ROM is that data on it cannot be erased. The WORM (Write Once–Read Many) technology is an effort to overcome this deficiency.

Central processing unit—The central brain or processor of the computer where timing, routing of data, and other decisions are made.

Chip—The basic hardware unit of microcomputer technology, made of silicon.

Circuit board—A board that contains a number of chips and controls a device such as a printer or modem, or houses the RAM and ROM (memory) of the computer.

Clone—A computer that emulates a more popular brand in order to capitalize upon the market.

Command language—An English-like computer language used with programs such as *dBase* to produce more sophisticated programs.

Compatible—*See* Clone above.

Compiler—A program that takes BASIC or other high-level language program and converts it into the machine code of the computer.

Co-processor—A second or additional central processing unit in a computer.

CP/M operating system—Control Program for Microprocessors was one of the first and most popular of the operating systems available for microcomputers. A large body of public domain software contributed to its popularity.

Crash—A total, and usually sudden, system failure.

CRT—Cathode Ray Tube, referring to the monitor or TV screen used for computer program display.

Cursor—Usually a flashing square pointing to where the next character on the computer screen will appear.

Dedicated—A program, telephone line, or other device used for a single purpose or function.

Default—Factory settings, hardware or software, which typically take over when the computer operator fails to make a conscious decision.

Desktop publishing—Creating camera-ready copy with the computer and printer, often entailing a laser printer for high-quality production. Also refers to simpler products produced on a dot matrix printer and programs such as *The Print Shop.*

Digital—"1"s and "0"s (digits), which are added upon into bytes to form computer words or characters, as opposed to the analog or continuous signal of the telephone lines.

DIP switch—Dual In-Line Package or the set of switches on a computer device that permit it to be used with a variety of computers. This flexibility is important because most manufacturers do not know what kind of computer their product will be used with later.

Disk—A small circular object on which data is stored and retrieved, and used in a disk drive. Also called diskette.

Disk drive—The mass-storage device that reads and writes on a disk. These data storage devices come in many sizes and types and may be built in or external to the computer.

Disk operating system—The master control program that manages the filing system and interfaces with the disk drives.

Documentation—The printed or online manuals that give the instructions for use of a program.

Download—To receive a program into a computer from a (usually) remote or distant computer. Opposite of "upload." The program can then be copied to disk for future use.

Duplex—Full duplex is simultaneous transmission of data in both directions, whereas half duplex is transmission in either direction but only one direction at a time.

Electronic mail—Sending messages electronically. May be sent locally through a bulletin board system or nationally through a nationwide network.

Encryption—A system for encoding data in a secret way so as to prevent its retrieval or use by another party.

Ergonomics—The comfort (or lack thereof) provided in the workstation, including seating, lighting, and climate.

Error message—Any message that the computer sends as a signal that something is wrong. Example: "Disk Full."

Font—Typeface.

Format—To initialize a disk for use by the computer.

Generic software—Software created for a wide variety of uses rather than dedicated to one use. Includes word processors, database managers, spreadsheets, etc. Opposite of a program which, for example, creates catalog cards exclusively.

Graphics tablet—An input device that allows the user to draw or trace objects that are then digitized for computer use.

Hacker—Originally a term used to describe a computer enthusiast, it now means someone who uses a computer for destructive purposes, such as crashing bulletin boards, invading mainframes illegally, and other mischievous acts.

Hardcopy—Printed computer data.

Hardware—The nuts-and-bolts parts of the computer that can be seen and felt, such as monitor, chips, keyboard, disk drives.

Hertz—A measurement of the speed with which the computer processes data. The greater the Hertz, the faster the computer.

Housekeeping—Maintenance programs or activities designed to keep a system up to working specifications.

Icon—Graphic representation of object on screen for quick identification of a computer function.

Integrated software—Software that does more than one thing, usually word processing, database management, spreadsheet, telecommunications, and graphics.

Interactive—Computer programs that require a human response. Noninteractive software (demonstration programs, for instance) will run without human intervention.

Interactive fiction—Roleplaying adventure games where the player takes the part of a character.

Joystick—The handheld stick used for computer games and sometimes as a menu control device.

Local area network—A system that connects computers for the sharing of data, files, electronic mail, and expensive peripherals.

Mainframe computer—A large computer usually requiring air conditioning and a special room and support, hence the name ''mainframe'' which refers to this support.

Memory—A computer's ability to store and hold data. To a large extent, determines its capabilities. Data may be stored internally in the computer's chips or externally on hard or floppy disk drives.

Microcomputer—A small desktop or home computer. The distinctions between different sizes of computers blurs as large ones decrease in size and small ones increase in power.

Minicomputer—A medium-range computer in both capability and memory.

Modem—From the words ''modulator'' and ''demodulator''; a device for translating the digital code of the computer into the analog code of the telephone line and back again. Two modems (one at each end) are required for two computers to communicate over the telephone. Computers can be directly connected without modems if they are close enough to connect with a cable.

Monitor—The screen that displays the computer's answers or data.

Mother board—The main circuit board to which all other circuit boards are connected. It houses the RAM, ROM, and CPU.

Multiplexing—A state in which a computer appears to be doing two things at once but is really doing two or more things very quickly.

Off-the-shelf software—Software written for a very specific use, not modifiable to any great extent.

Parallel transmission—One byte of data being sent eight bits simultaneously.

Parameter—A setting for baud rate, parity, line feeds, etc., that determines how a device or computer will act. These parameters may be changed by the operator under software control or, sometimes, under hardware control with DIP switches, but they always have factory settings (defaults).

Parity—A method for checking the accuracy of data transmission by adding up the data bits that must be either odd or even. If the proper addition is not made by the computer, the data is rejected and must be retransmitted.

Peripheral—Any device not part of the computer proper, whether internal or external to the computer housing. Peripheral devices include modems, printers, disk drives, and graphics tablets.

Printer—A device for printing out hardcopy of the computer results. Printers may be dot matrix, daisywheel, or laser.

Protocol—An agreed-upon method for data transmission that reduces the chance of error. For instance, if two computers are programmed to accept only incoming sets of data bit or signals that add up to an even number, one coming in as an odd number is judged incorrect and must be retransmitted (*see* Parity).

Public domain—Software without copyright restrictions.

RAMworks—A memory card for the Apple computer that adds large amounts of internal RAM memory to the system.

Random Access Memory—RAM is computer memory that changes as the computer uses it.

Read Only Memory—ROM is memory that already has a program stored on it. The computer can read this memory or stored information, but cannot change or add to it.

RS-232-C—A standard determining the interface between modems and computers.

Sector—A magnetically created rectangular area on a disk used by the computer to store, locate, and retrieve data.

Serial transmission—Data being sent between computers one bit at a time in single file.

Shareware—Copyrighted software that is freely distributed. If the user wishes to continue to use it, a license fee must be remitted to the owner of the software, as stipulated in the software itself.

Softcopy—Information sent to the computer screen, distinct from "hardcopy," which is printed out.

Software—The invisible part of the computer; the set of instructions that tells the hardware what to do with the data it receives.

Source code—Uncompiled program code that may be altered by users for their own purpose.

Spooler—A method of sending data to a buffer or storage area in order to free up the computer or other device. For instance, by sending a long file to a buffer, the computer may continue to function without waiting; by sending a second file to the print buffer, a line or queue is formed waiting for the printer to finish.

Spreadsheet—The electronic version of the accountant's pad. Formulas and data may be entered and the results calculated immediately. A second set of data or a change in any data element will result in a recalculation of the entire spreadsheet, making it possible to judge the effect of changes in budgets, for example, very quickly.

Supercomputer—The most powerful computer in existence at a given time.

Surge protector—A device that reduces harmful, momentary increases in electrical energy ruinous to computers.

Synchronous—Data transmission that is regulated by synchronized clocks in both the sending and receiving computers.

Sysop—A combination form of "system operator"; one who controls or has responsibility for maintenance of a computer system, either micro-, mini-, or mainframe computer.

Telecommunication—Communication over long distances, through either telephone lines, satellite, or other means.

Telecommute—The act of going to work at the terminal without having to go physically to the workplace.

Template—A form, electronic or paper, that represents work someone has prepared but that may be used over and over with different sets of data. An example is the spreadsheet in which formulas have been placed for creating a budget. Since any two businesses that use the same kind of budget can use the same formulas, they can use the same template.

Terminal—A place where people may interface with a computer, in the form of a keyboard, a monitor, or printer. The computer need not be present; it can be reached through the telephone lines with a modem or directly through cable (known as hardwiring) in a local area network.

Track—Concentric magnetic rings on a computer disk which, when divided into sectors, map out where data is stored on the disk by the computer. All disks come blank and must be formatted or initialized, which divides them into these magnetic tracks and sectors.

Upload—To accept data into a computer. The opposite of "download," which is to send data to another computer.

User group—Any group of people who get together for the purpose of exchanging information about computers, especially problem-solving. Such groups can host special events, such as speakers or hardware and software demonstrations, or get group discounts on computers and supplies.

Word processing—A software program that allows users to rearrange and revise text (sentences, words, etc.), without having to retype everything before hardcopy is produced. Often these programs come with "spellers," which check documents for suspect words (possibly misspelled words).

Workstation—An area that contains the necessary equipment (furniture, outlets, table, etc.) for work with a computer. Such places should have good lighting and comfortable seating (*see* Ergonomics above).

WORM (Write Once–Read Many)—A type of CD-ROM that allows for writing on CD that cannot be erased but that can be read as often as desired.

Bibliography: 101 Useful Books

Administration

Hernon, Peter, and McClure, Charles R., eds. *Microcomputers for Library Decision Making: Issues, Trends, and Applications.* Ablex, 1986.

Schuyler, Michael and Hoffman, Jake. *PC Management: A How-to-do-it Manual for Selecting, Organizing, and Managing Personal Computers In Libraries.* Neal-Schuman, 1990.

CD-ROM

Duggan, Mary Kay, ed. *CD-ROM in the Library Today and Tomorrow.* G. K. Hall, 1990.

Lambert, Steve, and Ropiequet, Suzanne. *CD-ROM: The New Papyrus.* Microsoft, 1986.

Nelson, Nancy Melin. *Essential Guide to the Library IBM PC: Library Applications of Optical Disk and CD-ROM Technology.* Meckler, 1987.

Nissley, Meta, et al. *CD-ROM Licensing and Copyright Issues for Libraries.* Meckler, 1990.

Sherman, Chris. *The CD-ROM Handbook.* McGraw-Hill, 1988.

Stewart, Linda, et al., eds. *Public Access CD-ROMs in Libraries: Case Studies.* Meckler, 1990.

Database Management

Beiser, Karl. *Essential Guide to dBase III+ in Libraries.* Meckler, 1986.

Buckley, Jo Ann. *Essential Guide to the Library IBM PC: Database Management Systems.* Meckler, 1986.

Bultema, Patrick. *The PC Mailing List Book.* Murach, 1990.

Hayman, Lynne, ed. *101 Uses of dBase in Libraries.* Meckler, 1990.

Tenopir, Carol, and Lundeen, Gerald. *Managing Your Information: How to Design and Create a Textual Database on Your Microcomputer.* Neal-Schuman, 1988.

181

Desktop Publishing

Bove, Tony, and Rhodes, Cheryl. *Desktop Publishing with PageMaker*. Wiley, 1987.

Crawford, Walt. *Desktop Publishing for Librarians*. G. K. Hall, 1990.

Johnson, Richard D., and Johnson, Harriett H. *The Macintosh Press: Desktop Publishing for Libraries*. Meckler, 1989.

Lucas, Andrew. *Desktop Publishing: Using PageMaker on the Apple Macintosh*. Halsted Press, 1987.

Murray, Katherine. *Using PFS: First Publisher*. Que, 1990.

Schaeffer, Mark. *Library Displays Handbook*. Wilson, 1991.

Schenck, Mary, and Benton, Randi. *The Official New Print Shop Handbook*. Bantam Books, 1990.

DOS

Doms, Dennis, and Weishaar, Tom. *ProDOS Inside and Out*. TAB Books, 1986.

Harriman, Cynthia W. *The MS-DOS - Mac Connection*. Brady, 1988.

Krumm, Robert. *Getting the Most from Utilities on the IBM PC*. Brady, 1987.

Murdock, Everett Errol. *DOS the Easy Way*. H.O.T. Press, 1988.

Electronic Bulletin Boards

Bowen, Charles, and Peyton, David. *The Complete Electronic Bulletin Board Starter Kit with RBBS-PC Software*. Software by Tom Mack. Bantam Books, 1988.

Dewey, Patrick R. *Essential Guide to Bulletin Board Systems*. Meckler, 1987.

Dewey, Patrick R. *National Directory of Bulletin Board Systems*. Annual. Meckler, 1991.

Hedtke, John V. *Using Computer Bulletin Boards*, MIS Press, 1990.

Moore, Cathy. *Bulletin Boards for Libraries*. Oryx, 1988.

Electronic Mail

Dewey, Patrick R. *EMail for Libraries*. Meckler, 1990.

Facsimile Transmission

Dewey, Patrick R. *FAX for Libraries*. Meckler, 1990.

Fishman, Daniel, and King, Elliot. *The Book of FAX: An Impartial Guide to Buying and Using Facsimile Machines*. Ventanna Press, 1988.

General Texts

Crawford, Walt. *Current Technologies in the Library: An Informal Overview*. G. K. Hall, 1988.

Helal, Ahmed H., and Weiss, Joachin W., eds. *Developments in Microcomputing: Discovering New Opportunities for Libraries in the 1990s*. Universitatsbibliothek, 1990.

Intner, Sheila S., and Hannigan, Jane Anne. *The Library Microcomputer Environment: Management Issues*. Oryx, 1988.

Handbooks

Costa, Betty, and Costa, Marie. *A Micro Handbook for Small Libraries and Media Centers*. 3rd ed. Libraries Unlimited, 1991.

Handicapped

Mates, Barbara T. *Library Technology and Physically Handicapped Patrons*. Meckler, 1991.

Hardware

Berliner, Don. *Managing Your Hard Disk*. Que, 1986.

Brumm, Penn. *The Micro to Mainframe Connection*. TAB Books, 1986.

Cummings, Steve, et al. *LaserJet IIP Essentials*. Peachpit Press, 1990.

Melin, Nancy Jean. *Essential Guide to the Library IBM PC: The Hardware Set-Up and Expansion*. Meckler, 1986.

Morrison, Chris, and Stover, Teresa S. *PC Care Manual: Diagnosing and Maintaining Your MS-DOS, CP/M or Macintosh System*. TAB Books, 1987.

Naiman, Arthur. *Macintosh Bible*. Goldstein & Blair, 1988.

Pfeiffer, Katherine Shelly. *The LaserJet Font Book*. Peachpit Press, 1990.

Pina, Larry. *Macintosh Printer Secrets*. Hayden, 1990.

Polly, Jean Armour, et al. *Essential Guide to Apple Computers in Libraries: Hardware Set-Up and Expansion*. Meckler, 1987.

Salkind, Neil J. *The Big Mac Book*. Que, 1989.

Sheldon, Thomas. *Hard Disk Management in the PC and MS DOS Environment*. McGraw-Hill, 1988.

HyperCard

Gluck, Myke. *HyperCard, HyperText, and HyperMedia for Libraries and Media Centers*. Libraries Unlimited, 1987.

Goodman, Danny. *The Complete HyperCard Handbook*. Bantam Books, 1987.

Local Area Networks

Apple Computer, Inc., Staff. Understanding Computer Networks. Addison-Wesley, 1989.
Desmarais, Norman, ed. *CD-ROM Local Area Networks: A User's Guide.* Meckler, 1990.
Marks, Kenneth, and Nielsen, Steven. *Local Area Networks in Libraries.* Meckler, 1991.
Wright, Keith. *Workstations and Local Area Networks for Librarians.* ALA, 1990.

Projects and Project Management

Dewey, Patrick R. *101 Microcomputer Projects to Do in Your Library.* ALA, 1990.
Lane, Elizabeth. *Microcomputer Management and Maintenance for Libraries.* Meckler, 1990.

Public Access

Dewey, Patrick R. *Public Access Microcomputers: A Handbook for Librarians.* 2nd ed. G. K. Hall, 1990.
Duke, John K., and Hirshon, Arnold. "Policies for Microcomputers in Libraries: An Administrative Model." *Information Technology and Libraries*, September 1986, 193.
Polly, Jean Armour. *Essential Guide to Apple Computers in Libraries.* Meckler, 1986.

Reference

Dewey, Patrick R. *Microcomputers and the Reference Librarian.* Meckler, 1989.

Software

Cargill, Jennifer, ed. *Integrated Online Library Catalogs.* Meckler, 1990.
Dewey, Patrick R. *Interactive Fiction and Adventure Games.* 2nd ed. Meckler, 1991.
Glossbrenner, Alfred. *Alfred Glossbrenner's, Master Guide to Free Software for IBMs and Compatible Computers.* St. Martin's Press, 1989.
Lawrence, Anthony. *Software, Copyright, and Competition: The "Look and Feel" of the Law.* Quorum Books, 1989.
Mace, Paul. *The Paul Mace Guide to Data Recovery.* Simon & Schuster, 1988.
Machalow, Robert. *Using Microsoft Excel.* Neal-Schuman, 1991.

Software Cataloging

Holzberlein, Deanne. *Computer Software Cataloging: Techniques and Examples.* Haworth Press, 1986.

Software Directories

Buckleitner, Warren. *Survey of Early Childhood Software*. High/Scope Press, 1989.

Desmarais, Norman. *Essential Guide to the Library IBM PC: Acquisitions Systems for Libraries*. Meckler, 1988.

Dewey, Patrick R. *Essential Guide to the Library Apple*. Meckler, 1987.

Dewey, Patrick R. *Essential Guide to the Library IBM PC: Generic Software for Library Use*. Meckler, 1985.

Dlug, Paul. *Microsoft Works 2.0: IBM Applications*. Windcrest Books, 1990.

MacGuide: The Complete Guide to Macintosh Software & Accessories, Delta Group, quarterly.

MacMenu Software Guide for Apple II Computers. Black Box Corporation, annual.

MacMenu Software Guide for Commodore Computers. Black Box Corporation, annual.

MacMenu Software Guide for IBM Computers. Black Box Corporation, annual.

MacMenu Software Guide for Local Area Networks. Black Box Corporation, annual.

MacMenu Software Guide for Macintosh Computers. Black Box Corporation, annual.

Miles, Susan Goodrich. *Essential Guide to the Library IBM PC: Library Application Software*. Meckler, 1986.

Spreadsheets and Statistics

Auld, Lawrence. *Electronic Spreadsheets for Libraries*. Oryx, 1986.

Hernon, Peter, et al. *Microcomputer Software for Performing Statistical Analysis: A Handbook Supporting Library Decision Making*. Ablex, 1988.

Telecommunications

Epler, Doris M. *Online Searching Goes to School*. Oryx, 1989.

Goldmann, Nahum. *Online Research and Retrieval with Microcomputers*. TAB Books, 1985.

Jack, Robert F. *Essential Guide to the Library IBM PC: Data Communications Going Online*. Meckler, 1987.

Viruses

Roberts, Ralph. *Compute!'s Computer Viruses*. Compute! Books, 1988.

Roberts, Ralph, and Kane, Pamela. *Compute!'s Computer Security*. Compute! Books, 1989.

Word Processing

Alderman, Eric. *Microsoft Word: The Complete Reference*. McGraw-Hill, 1988.

Hoffman, Paul. *Microsoft Word Made Easy*. McGraw-Hill, 1988.

LaPier, Cynthia B. *The Librarian's Guide to WordPerfect 5.0*. Meckler, 1990.

Index of Software

Patrick R. Dewey is the director of the Maywood (Illinois) Public Library District. He has served in the capacity since 1984. Before that, he was a reference librarian and branch librarian at the Chicago Public Library for ten years. Dewey holds an MLS from Wayne State University (Detroit). He has written 16 books, including the first two books in the 101 Micro series (published by ALA) and titles covering such diverse subjects as bulletin board systems, interactive fiction, comic book collecting, and fan clubs. He has published over 60 articles in library magazines and general computer magazines and has served as an associate editor of *Computers in Libraries*.